DISPOSABLE
EXPENDA

G. C. Rossi

Order this book online at www.trafford.com
or email orders@trafford.com

Most Trafford titles are also available at major online book retailers.

Printed in the United States of America.

ISBN: 978-1-4269-7036-8 (sc)
ISBN: 978-1-4269-7037-5 (e)

Trafford rev. 07/18/2011

 www.trafford.com

North America & International
toll-free: 1 888 232 4444 (USA & Canada)
phone: 250 383 6864 ♦ fax: 812 355 4082

TABLE OF CONTENTS

ACKNOWLEDGEMENTS

Thank you to the following people who encouraged my endeavors:

My husband, Ralph
My children, Gaby, Lynn, Karen, and Diana
Jennifer Bancroft
Penny Carter
The late Dr. Nathan Getzler
Dr. Harvey I. Halperin
Debbie Rozenberg

INTRODUCTION

This book is the recollection of my experiences. The people and places are how I remember them.

My most vivid memories of a normal life in our family was when my father was still living and my mother was badgering and henpecking. My parents had an arranged marriage to which my mother was an unwilling participant. Although our family life was stormy, as a child my life still seemed good.

The general population is sleepwalking into hospitals, unaware of what can happen. It is a cruel conspiracy, an agenda between doctors, pharmaceutical companies, and government. I am not crying wolf. I am a product of this conspiracy for I was a test subject back in the 1950's and 1960's.

Chosen to be part of a team of psychiatrists to evaluate whether Rudolf Hess, suspected of war crimes against humanity, was able to stand trial for his participation of crimes at Nuremburg, Dr. Ewan Cameron was certainly aware that atrocities were conducted and carried out by the Nazis. Yet, in the 1950's and 1960's, research and experiments initiated in Montreal, Canada, by Dr. Cameron were carried out in the name of science. He did not have to account for the limitless source of funds forwarded to the Allan Memorial Institute on his behalf.

1 Cameron – He became a witness to history in a big way, there in Nuremberg, as part of what he called "a clean wind to the prison house that was Germany". Hess was one of the first of the Nazi leaders brought to justice. (W.p.108)

Unsuspecting patients were used and abused through the use of experimental drugs and psychiatric treatment. Many were unwilling, but were nevertheless coerced into continuing with the drugs and the painful treatments. Few recuperated. Many were mentally and emotionally destroyed. This project of experimentation on mind control was the brainchild of Dr. Cameron. Like an untouchable, he always walked ahead in a group, not alongside the others. He was the nucleus. Everyone revolved around him. As chief and head of the department of psychiatry at the Allan Memorial Institute, the interns and resident doctors were his "soldiers." He commanded, they obeyed. Some objected, but many who may not always have accepted his methods kept silent and looked away. These "soldiers" were as responsible as if they themselves were the initiators. In silence they condoned what was happening.

Dr. Cameron scrutinized every idea that his co-workers presented and therefore maintained full control. He did not always personally carry out his own ideas, but had others report to him and do the "work." Today there are other Dr. Camerons in other hospitals. With the decline of animal testing and experiments, one wonders how new drugs and cures might be tested or discovered for ailments and diseases. It is highly possible that the past will continue to haunt other unsuspecting, innocent victims. The animal activists fight for the rights of animals. Who fights for the rights of humans? History does repeat itself.

.

Fact. I was the only woman in my family to have placenta problems during pregnancy, placenta previa, and placenta insufficiency. All three of my pregnancies were unusual and difficult. The first two were almost two months premature, and all three births were extremely traumatic and high risk. It is difficult not to imagine that these events may have been due to all the drugs I had systematically been given, during my experience at the Allan Memorial Institute (AMI) prior to my marriage.

I have not had hepatitis since I left the hospital in May 1962. In 1972, I did have a follow up liver biopsy and my physician at that time could not understand my medical history or the symptoms

I was still experiencing. At the time of this biopsy my liver was still tender and enlarged. Yet all the tests taken for hepatitis were negative, including the biopsy. Tests could not conclude that I ever had had hepatitis. How is it possible that these tests came out negative, considering I was diagnosed and treated at length for hepatitis at the Royal Victoria Hospital ten years prior?

In 1978 during a bout of the flu, I was prescribed an anti-nausea drug. This drug contained some stelazine. Soon after ingesting the medication, my eyes rolled up into my head, my tongue would not stay in my mouth, my upper and lower jaws were pulling in opposite directions at the same time, and my neck and back were arched. I had no control of my limbs. I was totally contorted, and the strain of these contortions was extremely painful for me. Having experienced these contortions twice before, I knew that I would remain in this state of pain for hours. I realized that what was happening was a side effect of stelazine combined with another drug in the flu medication. This was like my whole body having a "Charlie Horse" cramp. This time I did not panic and I was not frightened. Many years prior to this event when I was purposely injected with stelazine to produce similar symptoms, I was told that an antidote was available. At that time the difference was that doctors were testing to see what the time duration of the effects from the drug would be, so the antidote was not administered.

When a neighbour drove me to the emergency of the Jewish General Hospital, I was given an IV with an antihistamine. An antihistamine was the simple antidote to the medication that caused my contortions. I would take anything as long as I could shake this horrible effect. This was my last experience with stelazine and its horrible side effects.

Although I feel that the drugs have had physical negative effects on me and possibly my children, I am now living a fairly normal life.

CHAPTER 1

ENTRANCE

To understand the circumstances that presented me as a candidate for the ordeal that ensued when I was in my teens, I will have to start at the very beginning.

Although my parents of Italian origin were Canadian born, we still maintained the lifestyle of a typical immigrant family where sons, daughters, and grandchildren were all living together under one roof. We all lived together until I was almost six years old, and my sister was two. My mother resented having to live with her parents and was very happy when a rental house became available to us within the same area. Back in the forties, Montreal experienced a housing problem. Many young married couples continued to live with their parents, even if they were not of immigrant families.

It was not an easy task for my grandparents to have us live with them. They would often witness my mother's frequent outbursts of anger, which were mostly for no apparent reason. Marriage seemed to bring out the worst side of my mother's character, and she made it intolerable for everyone if things did not please her.

It was apparent that my father loved my mother and his children. Had he not loved us all he would have left the marriage, but he did not want to abandon his children. My mother was incapable of love but had a need to possess everything and everyone. She was a perfectionist, a highly manipulative, self centered, rigid, and severe person. This was a woman who should never have married nor borne children. To her, children were possessions that were to be always kept clean and tidy, still, and quiet, like ornaments displayed on a shelf. Children were definitely not to have any imagination. These were some of the fences of my early childhood.

I was a difficult and rebellious child and failed miserably when it came to meeting my mother's expectations. As a toddler I thought nothing of climbing onto the table and throwing raw eggs onto the floor, because the eggs looked like balls and were in a beautiful wire chicken basket. If a pair of scissors were in sight, I would cut the fringes off the hanging curtains to make spaghetti. One of my faux pas was that one day, when I found my father's toolbox, I took his hammer and the largest nails I could find and nailed all the nails in a row on the balcony in front of the door. That made it impossible for the door to open. I was very pleased with myself because I finally locked my mother in, and therefore away from me. Of course I was punished for my deed.

In her behaviour to me, my mother was physically and emotionally abusive, and she curbed all attempts of positive interference by my father or other family members. Her contention was, "This is my child, and no one else's business!"

My father on the other hand, was a loving, caring, and natural parent. He was a carpenter by trade who had an artistic flare. This made for a contentious mix at best. His passion was creating wooden toys and furniture. He opened up a world of many memorable hours broadening my horizons of imaginative play.

Some of the toys that stand out in my memory are the little wooden dolls waddling down a ramp, or a clown on a jumping tight rope. As I grew older, he made other toys, such as a beautiful wooden light blue carriage for my many dolls. Another wonderful toy was a beautiful red wagon with big wheels. I would either pull it, or kneel down with one knee and push it with my other foot. I would put my small shovel and bucket in the wagon so that I could go and dig in the sand box outside. My father seemed to know and understand that I needed this outlet to focus on imaginary play.

Europe was at war during the forties, and many Canadians enlisted to participate in the war effort. Men just seemed to evaporate out of society. In Montreal, in the "Mile-end" neighbourhood, it was a common nightly exercise to watch the newly enlisted men in parade, marching behind a brass band. During those years this was a recruiting method used by the armed services.

Those were exciting times for children, but for adults and parents it was an anxious and worrisome time. Every family was impacted. My father tried to enlist but was rejected due to a heart condition. However, his two brothers enlisted and fought in Europe. We were fortunate that they returned physically unscathed.

I must have been a parent's nightmare as a child. I remember digging myself out of the back yard, and wandering through the lane to sit on the steps of the Synagogue on the next street. It was wonderful to sit on those steps and to hear the prayers being sung inside. Another time I allowed myself into our neighbour's house while she was at work because I wanted to eat olives that she kept in her larder. Once I helped a small friend climb a tree to pick apples, only to be accused of theft. A few of us played hairdresser, which caused detrimental effects.

I had long hair that my mother kept in braids. I decided that I needed bangs, so with a nice set of scissors, and a friend to look out for adults, we sat underneath a dark balcony and "voila," off went the hair above my forehead. I must have been quite a sight. My mother let out a blood-curdling scream and cried fiercely when she saw me. One day, after tolerating too many of my terror shenanigans, and no longer able to cope, in her frustration my own mother locked me into the dark cold and damp shed out back where the rats lived. My screams were so loud that the entire neighbourhood heard the racket, and eventually, in fear, my mother let me out because the neighbours threatened to call the police.

My father never experienced my outrageous childhood antics. This was partially due to the fact that he was always working during the day. My mother bullied him and prevented him from feeling comfortable being at home. Eventually his role in the household was gradually diminished. This forced him to leave the house every evening after supper.

When my father was around we would be together. We had a different relationship, and there are pleasant memories I have of him. We would draw together, read, and hang out. On many summer evenings my father took me to the park, whistling along the way, while carrying me on his shoulders. He also enjoyed taking me to listen to the brass band playing at the bandstand in the park. Afterwards we would go to eat ice cream and watch the fireworks at the park. We also enjoyed trips to the beach. We often went with his friends and their families for picnics, trips that would seldom include my mother. She did not enjoy relaxing in the sun or eating a picnic lunch on a blanket on the shore, while other people had fun splashing around in the water. These were very happy times for me.

One of the lasting memories I have of my father is the nightly ritual we had together. I would wake every night with the need to go to the bathroom. However, because my mother had threatened me with the "boogie man" underneath my bed, I did not dare step out off the bed until the light of day. I ended up calling out for my father and he always and very naturally came to my rescue. My father carried me on his back to the bathroom every night up until the day he died. My father always made me feel safe.

In 1947 I started afternoon kindergarten class. One day, just before leaving for school, my mother threw a tantrum and kept insisting that she was dying of a heart attack. This was such a traumatic feeling for me, envisioning my mother dying at any moment. My grandmother and aunt, who were at home, did not acknowledge her tantrum. She soon regained her composure and I was brusquely rushed off to school.

Shortly after being dropped off at school I ran home. I arrived home before my mother did and refused to go back. I could not leave her because of the fear that she would die. I was traumatized by her antics. This was one of the many ploys she used to convince people to do things for her.

It was 1948 and the war was over. Soldiers had returned and people were trying to resume normal lifestyles. More men were working again and housing soon became available. Shortly before my sixth birthday, my parents found and rented a house very close to everyone we knew. We moved from my grandparent's home to the new house. This was the first time that I was away from my grandmother, who often consoled me after one of my mother's many outbursts. Now I was on my own with my mother, and had to endure her daily torments.

I spent the time from May until September mostly playing out doors. There were some children living across the street and we became friends. We roller-skated together, played tag, hide and go seek, and hopscotch on the sidewalk. On cloudy and rainy days we played house indoors with our dolls at my new friend Doreen's house. Sometimes I would wander to my grandmother's or my Godmother's home. I loved them, and they always returned my affection. They were always happy to see me. Everyone I loved lived close by and it was easy to go from one house to another without fear. Children played outdoors unsupervised for hours, and parents never feared that harm would come to their children. It was a safe time.

During that summer my social life was temporarily interrupted by a case of mumps, and I was housebound until it was sure that I was no longer contagious. Unfortunately for my mother, she too was inconvenienced by my illness. She found it difficult to be with me and have me indoors. I interfered with her daily routine.

Sewing was her passion, and my mother filled most of the day sewing on her valued machine and listening to the radio. Her treasured machine took up most of the available space in our small kitchen.   She sewed all of our clothing, from underwear to winter coats, always creating a carpet of different coloured threads and small pieces of fabric all over the floor.   The kitchen table was used as the work area, and the cloth, pins, and needles were removed when it was time to prepare our meals, only to be returned again after the meal was over.

In September I started grade one.   There were several children on my street going to the same school, so we all walked to and from school together. Being in school made me feel that I was growing up. I was learning how to read and I had great pleasure trying to read, picturing the stories as I read. It was also satisfying to draw and colour and have some of my endeavors on the wall in the classroom for all to see.

My father's involvement in this house was not a welcome one. Early every morning he would leave for work only to return home for supper to an unhappy and combative wife.   With her behavior, my mother was systematically pushing him out of our lives.   Every meal would end with an argument that sent my father out to spend his evenings with others. He would return when all the lights in the house had been turned off. Most of the time I was still awake when he returned, and because I suffered leg pains, he would rub my legs before he went to bed.

Bedtime was at 7:00 p.m. for my sister and 7:30 p.m. for me. I had always had problems sleeping, adding to my mother's distress. I would lay awake in bed and after a while call out, either to have something to drink or to go to the bathroom. This would annoy my mother to no end. She had to accompany me whenever I had to get out of bed. Her threat of the boogieman awaiting underneath my bed to pull my legs if I stepped out of bed frightened me.

Whenever things did not work in her favour, my mother's frustration would end with her beating me with my grandfather's shaving strap. This strap was made of two heavy pieces of thick leather held at the top by a metal clip. My legs and arms were always covered in bruises and welts. I was embarrassed to go to school with these battle scars because everyone could see my shame.

My mother kept yelling at me, telling me that I was bad. Her favourite threatening phrase was that I was so bad that she would send me to reform school. She just could not cope with me.

I had a good imagination and within boundaries would explore the neighbourhood. I knew all the neighbours and they knew me. I enjoyed books, and loved drawing and colouring on the blackboard in my bedroom with the coloured chalk my father had given me. To my mother these were frivolous efforts and a waste of time. She would have preferred me to keep quiet, sit still, and sew.

One sunny spring afternoon after school, I was suddenly taken to a barber and my long hair was cut extremely short. I cried when I saw the result. I felt very strange with this chopped haircut. That was on Friday. Two days later, after having eaten lunch, my mother asked my father to take my sister to our grandmother's house. Shortly after my father left, a lady whom I had never seen before arrived. There was a little packed suitcase at the front door, and my mother said that we would be going on a long streetcar ride with this friend. The mysterious lady was in fact a missionary with the United Church of Canada.

After having taken three streetcars and a bus, we arrived at our final destination, a big brown building facing a park. This was "The Children's Home" in Lachine, and it was a missionary project of the United Church of Canada.

Inside the building, I was taken to a playroom and while I played, my mother signed forms in an office. Then she and the missionary who had brought me here left. No one said good-bye and I did not know that I would be left there. I was like an unwanted animal being returned to the animal shelter. I started to cry when I realized that my mother had left, and could not understand why she deserted me.

There were two dormitories on the second floor. One was for the girls and one was for the boys. Before supper, a housemother took me upstairs with my suitcase and showed me to a bed, and then I was taken into the dinning room to meet everyone. For the next few months I cried and could not eat properly. I also had to adapt to different foods. At home I was accustomed to eating Italian style meals. At the Home the food was bland and basic meat, potatoes, and rice. At home, I enjoyed eating an Italian dish called risotto, but here I could not swallow the tasteless boiled rice that made me gag.

At the Home, all the children went to the public school in the area. I was the youngest one at the Home and still in grade one. This was a different school and I had already surpassed the school curriculum, so I only attended the morning class. Every afternoon I was left on my own.

Within the first few weeks I befriended a retired policeman who worked the cross walk in front of the school. I was always crying and wanted to go home. I would implore him to please help me go back home. All I had to do was take the streetcar, a bus, and then two more streetcars. This man was familiar with the Children's Home and he would always take me into the candy store to try and calm me before taking me back to the Home.

One housemother would rock me in her lap or play classical music on the piano to try and console me. One of the piano pieces she played I recognized as Tchaikovsky's June Barcarole.　Now every time I hear this piece, it brings me back to that six-year-old sitting in a rocker, being consoled in the arms of a kind stranger.

The boys at the Home were in Cubs and the girls were in Brownies.　I was too young to be a Brownie, so every week for the hour that they went to their meetings, I was left alone at the Home.　It was still light so I would wander outside across the street in the park. It was safe and quite a nice park with monkey bars and a few wading pools. At the Home we were free to wander, provided we returned when the whistle was blown.　We were free to play with the neighbourhood children but many of their parents would not allow them to play with us.

Months later my father finally found out where I had been taken, and at the end of the school year he came to take me home.　My mother was very upset that I was back home and as soon as she could manage it she proceeded to send me away to a summer camp. This time she told me that she and my sister would join me, but at the last minute after boarding the bus, she again disappeared and left me with strangers. This was how she coped with me, by keeping me away.

In September of 1949 I was back to my previous school, but I was now in grade two. I was not expected at the school and my grade one teacher did not recognize me. I had changed. I had become withdrawn and much thinner, and instead of long braids, my hair was bobbed. I did not resemble the child who had been in her grade one class. Eventually a classroom was found for me and I began the second grade.

CHAPTER 2

LOST DREAMS

Back in Montreal of 1850, there was a young immigrant Scottish banker who, as a gift for his young Scottish bride, had a three-storey mansion built on several acres of land. Just shy of a hundred years later in 1948, my grandfather bought this mansion. It was a huge brick and stone building surrounded by a magnificent English garden, with purple lilac trees and pink wild rose bushes. The large elm and maple trees were old and majestic, and when in foliage stood as tall centurions protecting the house.

The walls of the house were three feet thick and the space within the walls was filled with stone for insulation. This kept the house very cool in the summer and warm in the winter. The enormous behemoth wood and coal-burning furnace that was in the boiler room provided heat and hot water during the severe and cold winter months. When the furnace was off during the hot summer months, an auxiliary gas heated water tank provided hot water for the entire house.

My grandfather wanted the family to live together again and eventually my mother agreed to this arrangement. We were three families living under one roof, my grandparents, my uncle with his family, and my parents, sister, and myself. This house was divided so that we could all live comfortably and separately in privacy without interfering with each other, yet we were still able to interact together when we wanted. All the children had the freedom of the house, and the pleasure of having playmates with whom to play and explore throughout this enormous building.

This was an ideal house for children with plenty of imagination. All the rooms were very spacious, but the windowsills were the favourite play areas for us all. They were deep and wide with curtains away from the windows, making them resemble a miniature stage. Whenever we played indoors, we were privileged to have physical and emotional space for endless hours of imaginative play. The bedroom closets were large and spacious, thus providing plenty of space for clothing, toys, and fantastic and comfortable hiding nooks. Playing on the windowsills with our dolls, making up funny skits for each other, or playing hide and seek kept us occupied, and gave our parents comfort knowing that we were not getting into mischief. We had a huge windowless cubby over one of the back stairwells that became a wonderful hiding place for children. This house provided all of us with a lifetime of happy childhood memories. These were very happy and safe times.

My family lived upstairs on the third storey. The long oak staircase leading to our upstairs apartment had an enticing and magnificent large oak banister, inviting many enjoyable trips sliding down which we children thoroughly relished. Each slide was an imaginary trip flying down a hill.

Living in Montreal in the 1950's, children went to the school closest to where they lived. This was before out-of-area school buses were provided. My school was approximately two miles away and children were encouraged to walk the distance. When it was not cold, raining, or snowing, I would walk home with a group of my friends rather than take the bus. It was still a safe era for children to be out of doors. People had more trust in one another, and children could slowly wander home without their parents having to worry.

One cold and rainy November morning in 1952, my father drove me to school. Sometimes my father would drive me to school, especially if the weather was cold and wet, because otherwise I would have a fifteen-minute walk to the bus. I enjoyed these mornings with my father, for they seemed to brighten the dull atmosphere of those humid and gray autumn days. When we arrived at school I gave my father a kiss and we said good-bye, not knowing that it was the last time that I would see him alive. That kiss was a parting kiss forever.

That Monday afternoon, after my last goodbye to my father, it was still raining and cold. When school ended I took the bus with a group of friends to the end of the bus line. My friends, all of us 10 years of age, lived in this area, but I lived a little further on across the highway. I walked the rest of the way home alone. I could see our house from the highway. Three cars that were parked in our driveway: our car, a police cruiser, and another car that I did not recognize. Anxiety set in, adrenaline rushed through me, and the darkness that would soon mark my youth began to seep into my core. I ran the rest of the way home with a sense of urgency and panic. That day is bookmarked as one of the most horrific memories of my life.

When I finally arrived at my house, my uncle was standing outside the back entrance. He was unusually quiet and stood rigidly holding his young daughter. I remember at that moment thinking, "Why isn't he at work?" Inside the house, I discovered my mother, my little sister, my grandparents, and my aunt all sitting at my grandmother's kitchen table. Everyone had a strange expression. Only my aunt had enough courage to tell me not to go upstairs, but to sit and stay close beside her. An icy sensation sank to the pit of my stomach. It was eerie and I could not understand why everyone was at home in the middle of the afternoon. I had difficulty understanding why everyone who had once provided me with security was now behaving so strangely. Nothing seemed normal or comforting at this time in my life. This was the beginning of my downward spiral, both emotionally and physically.

Two policemen and the family doctor soon came downstairs from our apartment. For what seemed like an eternity, oddly no one spoke. I still did not know what this solemn and quiet gathering was all about. When the people left, I was finally told that my father had died of a sudden heart attack earlier that afternoon. We now had to wait for the coroner so that my father's body could be removed from his room upstairs. The father who had cheerfully kissed me good-bye that morning now lay lifeless in his room.

For a ten-year-old child this experience was surreal. This was definitely a sad realization for me, and I remember feeling a sense of loneliness. I felt empty, lost, and insecure. What did this mean for my family and my future? Life was about to take a new route, one that would prove to be most challenging for even the strongest personality!

I was in shock. It was incomprehensible that my poppa was well this morning and dead this afternoon. How could this happen? He did not look ill. He did not even have a cold, so why did he die? Why? Why? Why? Life can be so unfair. My world crumbled and my life was shattered. I was in shock and disbelief.   It was not true. This could not have happened to my poppa.

The emotional impact of my father's death did not affect me until several days after the funeral. It was then that I suddenly realized that death was very final. I began to feel the emptiness of my existence and became frightened and insecure. Fever, a lack of appetite, and depression kept me away from school for almost a month. When I was well again I still was not ready to see or speak to anyone, and I wanted to be left alone. I hurt inside and did not know how to make the hurt go away. Eventually I had to go back to school. My apprehension about being with other people was enormous. Now I was different. No longer was I a carefree ten-year-old child, but the only one in my class without a father. How would my school friends react? What would the teacher say?

Slowly I adapted to my status at school. My teacher had told the children that my father had died. This probably prevented them from asking

The eleven-year-old intermediate students had to complete grade seven. Grade eight and up were senior students who remained at Summerhill House until the age of sixteen, when they were required to leave. It was a mystery where they went after that.

Many of the girls at Summerhill House were not scholastically inclined, so it was not unusual for a ten-year-old to be in the third grade. At that time most of the institutionalized children lagged behind in the school curriculum, probably because of our individual circumstances of being emotionally scarred.

At the turn of the century, prior to being a home, Summerhill had been an asylum. This gray foreboding building was on the corner of Guy and Summerhill Avenues. This was between McGregor Street and Sherbrooke Street and connected Guy Street to Redpath Street. The date and the word "asylum" were etched in the glass window over one of the dormitory doors. All the girls living at this home experienced an odd feeling going through these doors, knowing that the predecessors whose spaces they now occupied were once considered "the insane". Summerhill House became my dwelling place until I was fifteen years old. I considered it a prison.

The girls at Summerhill constituted a melting pot of nations and religions. Prejudice was not tolerated, but it was not even an issue for us. We all had something in common. We all shared similar experiences of having come from broken homes, carried severe emotional scars, and lacked the warmth and love one naturally receives when living in a family environment. Secular and religious education were provided both to the neighbourhood community children and residents of the Home. Although we went to school with regular children, due to a strict "Home" schedule, we were not permitted to make friends or have contact with them outside of the classroom. This kept us separate from the rest of the children and left us with the feeling that we were different. This kept our feelings of rejection constant and ever present.

We all had to adapt to the social rejection from our classmates along with the detached and indifferent treatment from the staff at the Institution.

We were the "Institution Children." Due to our individual circumstances, people believed that our histories were suspicious. We were possibly a bad influence for "normal" children. We shunned children were underprivileged, undesirable, and socially unworthy.

The four-storey Summerhill House building had an enormous attic that was used for storage. At the beginning of every season, a few girls would be treated to a trip to the attic to choose clothes that were stored there in large tea crates. This was an event we all looked forward to, hoping that we would be one of the few chosen to find and try on new pieces of clothing. As exciting as choosing a new wardrobe was, very little of the clothing was new.

To get to the attic was an adventure in itself, and we all anticipated every trip with great excitement. We would go up into the extremely small, four-by-four foot antiquated cage elevator. It clanged and creaked the entire duration of the twelve seconds it needed to reach each floor. When it reached the landing it chugged, then sighed. It was much faster climbing the four flights of stairs, but we all enjoyed the novelty of the squeaky cage elevator. We still had to climb the last flight of stairs to get to the attic because the elevator only went to the fourth floor.

The fourth floor had a widow's tower that over-looked the area south east of Montreal and the St. Lawrence River. A forest of large trees surrounded the house, which was not easily seen from the bottom of the hill except in autumn and winter when the trees were without leaves. The girls of Summerhill House always thought that it looked haunted, especially in the autumn when all the trees had lost their leaves. It was an eerie looking house on top of that steep hill.

On the fourth floor were the widow's tower that was used only by the seamstress, and the one windowless detention room. Here the headmistress of the Home had her living quarters. This was a dreary and dark area into which one rarely ventured. The dormitories for the girls were on the second and third floors. These floors were much brighter but somewhat cooler than the others due to the many and overly large windows. The Housemothers, provided with room and board at the Home, had rooms on either the second or third floors. The kitchen and night staff had separate apartments over the kitchen. The kitchen was downstairs at the back of the house. The cloakroom, the laundry area, the storeroom, and the janitor's quarters were all in the basement. The main floor was where we spent our eating and leisure hours, and the only floor on which we were really permitted to spend time.

The headmistress was a red headed maiden lady of Scottish ancestry. We feared and yet respected her at the same time. Some of the girls had already experienced the wrath of her temper, which was as fiery as her red hair. When angered, she would lecture in a very loud tone making sure that we understood that consequences were to follow. She was a firm believer in rules and regulations, and she made sure to rule Summerhill House with a firm hand.

Religion was a very important part of our educational and moral growth at Summerhill House, and it was understood that we all needed religions guidance. Living in an upscale area, there were many religious institutions from which to choose. The headmistress allowed us that freedom of choice, as long as we attended weekly religious services at any of the congregations within the vicinity. Many of us tried different churches or prayer houses until we could settle on the one that we preferred to attend. After visiting a few of the churches with some of the girls, I came across one church that really caught my interest. It was the Erskine and American United Church, which had a fabulous organ. I loved music and this made me feel calm, relaxed, and at peace, feelings which were foreign at Summerhill.

It was during my time as an "inmate" at Summerhill that I discovered that the simple little things we all do freely, without restriction, were forbidden and unacceptable. Entering a dormitory, going to a different floor, or even stepping outside the gate was not permitted. If caught, the infraction was considered an offense, one that would lead to harsh and extreme consequences. There was constant supervision. Every minute of the day was accounted for, and we had to adhere to a strict schedule. We were permitted only so many minutes going to and coming from school.

If we did not conform to the set timetable we were punished.

Punishment was a thirty-minute penalty for every misdemeanor accrued during the week, resulting in a reduction of the allotted time permitted to visit with our respective families on Saturdays and Sundays. Children of the same family were not always permitted the same amount of time to visit with parents, due to their accrued misdemeanors. These were some of the draconian rules and regulations of the Home, rules that were feared and obeyed. I often fell victim to the harsh punishments. It was not difficult to be accused of a misdemeanor at Summerhill.

CHAPTER 3

A FINE BEGINNING

After being widowed for five years, my mother finally had a boyfriend. It was the winter of 1957. My sister and I also liked him and for us, the prospect of our mother having a husband meant that we could live in a house like a real family again. Now we felt hope.

Since the death of my father five years ago, I had been living at Summerhill House for four years, the place I considered a prison. My sister joined me at Summerhill when she was eight years old. Her experience was so different from mine. We could not have been more polar opposite, a trait we still carry in our adult lives. For her, Summerhill House provided the ideal environment. My sister flourished in isolation. She preferred to be alone and read rather than to play and integrate with others. It is possibly a result of the way she was raised by our mother. From the moment she was born, my mother had always kept my sister apart from my cousins and me, so she considered these years at the Home a time that shaped and encompassed her childhood. My prison was her sanctuary. Finally my dream had become a reality. My sister and I were leaving this prison to go home to our mother.

I was homesick the entire time that I spent at Summerhill House. I missed being at home and living in a regular house like the other children. Most of all I missed going to my grandmother for hugs. I missed having the freedom to go outside or to walk into any room in the house without being punished. Having a cookie or taking something out of the refrigerator was impossible and most forbidden. Visiting a school friend after school, or having her over, was not permitted either. Everyday common events, accepted unconsciously and guilt free for other youngsters, were not conventional for the children of Summerhill House. However, now because of my mother's boyfriend, my sister and I believed it would be possible to live at home again, far away from the restrictions of the orphanage. For me, it was the end of a long prison sentence.

In retrospect, although Summerhill House was a home for underprivileged girls, it provided opportunities to which otherwise we would not have been exposed. Every six months we were given regular dental care and yearly medical examinations. Through the kindness of various benevolent groups, such as the Kiwanis, we were exposed to Cultural activities. These included Children's Concerts, monthly movie nights featuring current movies, the circus, the Ice Follies, and live theatre. An art teacher and an arts and craft teacher were regular part-time staff. We were exposed to much more than the average child of that time.

At the end of June, on my fifteenth birthday, I left Summerhill House. That was the best present I could ever have wished to receive. It was a wonderful surprise to be going home to the big house, to my grandparents, family, and cousins, all of whom I missed terribly.

During the past four years I had spent at Summerhill, I had accumulated very few items. When I found out I was going home, it was not time consuming nor difficult to gather up all my belongings. I was given a small cardboard box where everything I owned was packed, and I was ready to leave within twenty minutes. Anyone leaving Summerhill House never had advance notice, for we were simply told to pack our belongings in a small box, and off we went. It was a very clean and sterile process that finalized our existence at Summerhill, without empathy or warmth. This was the standard procedure. There was no fuss and no long good-byes. Whenever someone left, a few of the girls would often cry, upset that a companion would not be seen again. We were all an appendage to each other, a security to the same affliction. Anyone leaving was disrupting this security and some of the girls felt this to be a personal rejection.

The summer of 1957 went by quickly. During the second week of July I had an appendectomy, and while I was recuperating at home, I started to contact old school friends I knew from before going to Summerhill. We were all in high school now and all of my friends were going to Mount Royal High School. It was then that I decided I would also transfer from the Girls High School downtown, where the Summerhill girls were attending, to join my previous friends at their school in the town of Mount Royal. It made more sense because it was also closer to my home.

A few months passed and my mother decided to move closer to her work, a place that was within walking distance of my sister's elementary school. She was planning to get married, so she thought that it would also be best to begin a new marriage in a different house. Our new apartment was in the northwest area of Park Extension, on the border of the town of Mount Royal. It was a nice area, closer to my friends, closer to the bus, and closer to the schools. At the Summerhill dormitories, I had to share space with anywhere from four to sixteen girls. Now, having to share a room with my sister, I was still provided with more space and privacy than I had become accustomed to in the dormitories. Life was sweet!

Our evenings at home were spent on homework and various hobbies, such as sewing, doing puzzles or artwork, listening to music and stories on the radio, or watching television. On one such evening the television was on. My mother was at her sewing machine sewing a garment, my sister was reading one of her favourite stories, and I was doing some artwork. It was a calm and peaceful evening at home. Eventually my young sister needed to go to bed, and my mother and I quietly and very happily continued with our hobbies.

Suddenly the front door of our apartment flung open with a horrific smashing sound against the wall. It was my mother's fiancé. He looked like a wild animal, and even today in my mind I can recall the look he had on his face. His thinning brown hair was messy and stood straight as though charged with electricity. He was mumbling and babbling incoherently. We could not understand what he was trying to say. It was obvious that he was quite inebriated. I had never seen him or anyone else in that state before. His irrational behavior frightened me, so I ran to the telephone and attempted to call my uncle for help.

It was then that my mother's boyfriend grabbed the scissors that were on the sewing machine, picked them up, and charged towards me. My mother let out a frightened scream that alarmed our neighbours. They immediately ran in from the apartment across the hallway, just in time to prevent the unthinkable from happening. This man in his uncontrolled state was intent on stopping me from making my phone call. He might have been successful had it not been for our neighbours. The wild man dropped the scissors and ran out. Our neighbour's wife took me back to her apartment where I spent the night, while he remained with my mother and sister until my uncle arrived. Although my mother never filed charges against this would be attacker, we thankfully never saw that man again, and carried on living our lives as best as we could.

This was a traumatic experience for us. We were all in shock. I was so affected that I could not speak. I remember feeling cold, and I shivered and shook uncontrollably. It was another one of those dark moments in my life. I witnessed my hopes of a new family shatter and disappear, a lost dream from which I would take a long time for me to recover. Soon after this horrifying experience, I went to stay with my mother's sister and her family. Living with a family gave me some sense of stability and security, and helped me again feel somewhat normal again.

We never did see that violent man again. I do not know what happened to him after that night, whether he abused alcohol regularly, or if that was an isolated incident. Contact with him was severed forever. We thought that he might have felt embarrassed about his behaviour, or maybe he had a severe drinking problem and decided that with this affliction was not ready for the commitment of a ready-made family. In any event it was distressing for all of us, especially my mother. Sadly, this was her one and only attempt at a second marriage.

My Aunt lived across from Montreal on the North Shore of the St. Lawrence River. Often, after a heavy rainfall or a big storm, it was common for the river to crest and flood the surrounding area. Cases of hepatitis were often reported in that area when the river flooded. The people living on the shoreline were frequently advised to boil the drinking water until the river level subsided. It was a habit we all maintained and respected.

During my time with my Aunt, I experienced a prolonged period of illness. It was a matter of months since I had been feeling well. Fever, pain, stomach cramps, and nausea made me return home to my mother. Odours in general made me feel sick to my stomach. The family doctor said that it was stomach flu, but this flu seemed to linger longer than normal. The nausea would not subside, the retching and vomiting resulted in a poor appetite, and I experienced massive weight loss. What was going on with me? I could not understand why I was so sick.

By winter my pallour was a chalky yellow and I began to vomit blood. This was definitely more than stomach flu. Seeing blood, my already worried mother began to panic. There was a snowstorm on that particular night and it was impossible to get a taxi. In desperation my mother called the police.

The two heavyset police officers who answered my mother's distress call arrived at the front door of our apartment building in a black police cruiser. Spotting the red light flashing on the roof of the cruiser instantly attracted the intense interest of the other tenants in our building. Apartment doors opened and slowly squeezed shut as the officers loudly ran up the stairs to our third floor apartment.

Hastily my mother and I, accompanied by the two officers, descended three flights of stairs. We exited the building and went into the black police cruiser. My sister stayed with our neighbours. All the while peering eyes followed us from the windows facing the street. The four doors of the cruiser slammed shut and we sped off into the cold and snowy night to a hospital.

This was a December winter night and Montreal was in the midst of a major snowstorm. The heavy storm was blanketing the city with a soft cover of snow, as though in preparation of the approaching festive holiday season. The silhouette of bright streetlights peeking through the falling snowflakes was beautiful, but driving through the thick mass of snow was slow and treacherous. It was during this storm the kind police officers drove us to the emergency of the Royal Victoria Hospital. The beginning of another nightmare for me began unfolding.

The Royal Victoria Hospital (RVH) complex was a collection of tightly clustered and extremely large gray granite buildings. They were connected by long dark corridors and spread over the southeast slope of Mount Royal Mountain. Built during the reign of Queen Victoria, it was fittingly named The Royal Victoria in her honour. A large gray stone statue of Queen Victoria stood in front of the main entrance.

In 1958, the RVH was an English teaching hospital that also served as a teaching facility for McGill University. It was the period of time prior to the end of the Duplessis era, and the beginning of the era of Jean Lesage, the man who became the next Premier of Quebec.

The federal government had gone from a long Liberal–held Party in power ending with the Honourable Louis St. Laurent, to a Conservative–lead power, headed by the Honourable John Diefenbaker, and then back again to the Liberals with the Honourable Lester B. Pearson as Prime Minister of Canada. Little did I know then how this series of political unrest and exchange would entangle and affect my life forever!

The Women's Medical Ward was at that time in the east wing off the main entrance on the second floor of the hospital. Facing Peel Street, it overlooked the McGill campus and the downtown core of Montreal. Day and night, regular traffic noises, combined with the constant abrasive wailing sirens of ambulances and police cruisers, were annoying and distressing. These buildings were not soundproof so that street noises carried and resonated throughout the entire hospital. There was not a single area that did not produce an echo. The very high ceilings tended to create a sort of echo chamber, which amplified the noise level tremendously.

The long and narrow medical ward, with its very high ceiling, featured fifteen large iron-post beds lined up on either side of the room. A large draughty window separated each bed. The terrazzo and dull-coloured battleship linoleum floors were always cold. Patient capacity was thirty. The beds were always filled. The facility was limited to two latrines at the end of the ward, one on each side.   One lone bathtub meant to accommodate all patients was located at the end of the ward next to one of the latrines. A visit to the washroom was a difficult and frustrating exercise for patients because it always entailed a very long walk.

Entering the ward, one immediately faced the nurse's station at the front. It was close to the corridor and enabled the staff to see and hear everything.   Behind the nurse's station were a few other rooms.   These rooms were reserved for special patients or for treatments. Adjacent to the nurse's station was the kitchen, with its continuous clatter of dishes, pots, and pans. The ever-present aroma of cooking was constantly permeating the air.   This daily barrage from the kitchen, which continued from early morning to the evening, was an additional nauseating discomfort to many patients, including myself.   It must have been quite an accomplishment for any medical staff to work in this archaic ward, considering the unrelenting noises and the sick reactions of the patients to the food smells.   This was definitely an uncommon environment.   It was, one would imagine, a place filled with terrible disruption for both the sick and the healing.

The constant rotation of new patients kept the nurses at maximum workload. The stress of the work in turn increased the irritability of the working staff. Due to this stress, decisions were made hastily. At times the ward was in complete chaos. The caring and concern of the young student nurses brought a glimmer of kindness and hope to this gloomy and hopeless environment. Young girls in starched uniforms, striped blouses, and white aprons, were the "probies", easily identified as our angels of mercy.

The school of nursing accepted students after graduation from high school. The average age of these young students was seventeen, and for the majority this was their first time away from home. In Quebec during the 1950's, student nurses were required to live in the hospital residences. This was imperative because student nurses were often expected to be available when needed on an on-call basis until 7:00 p.m. These young girls related that even though they were tired after grueling twelve-hour shifts, they would often stay up late into the night quizzing each other about their studies.

Doctors and nurses had little time if any to relax. Private or semi-private accommodations were not available. The RVH was not originally built with privacy in mind, but rather was built for the functional services and well being of the sick. Patients were at the mercy of the staff, and the staff was continuously under scrutiny of all the patients. This was where I would spend the next five to six weeks of my life. It was the ending of an old year with hopes of a new beginning, and a new beginning without hope for the future.

CHAPTER 4

INITIATION

It was December of 1958. After spending a long, noisy, and restless night, as well as the better part of the day in the emergency room, a bed in the medical ward finally became available for me. I was taken to the second floor on a stretcher and wheeled to a bed. There I lay in the middle of the room, on the East side of the ward facing the northern part of University Street, where the sun only shone in the early morning. Although the ward was lined with windows, it was not a very bright room.

Very sick people were in beds on both sides of this ward. Two constables stationed at the end of one bed served as full-time companions to a young woman who had attempted suicide the night before. Another young woman with skin the colour of iodine was in the next bed moaning and groaning and obviously in severe pain. Later that night she died of a liver disease. I learned that this woman left behind a family with two young children.

From the opposite side of the room came the sound of the constant grinding and gurgling of a suction machine, which was used to try to save the life of a cancer victim. Another woman, whose body was so puffed and swollen that she looked like a marshmallow, was afflicted by a glandular disorder. I do not remember much about that woman. A few months later, I would again see her at the Allan Memorial Institute (AMI), a place to which I would yo-yo back and forth from the RVH in the next three and a half years.

A middle-aged woman was rehabilitating from a stroke. She was paralyzed on one side of her body and was having daily physiotherapy to help her regain some mobility. Even though her speech was slurred, this woman could make herself understood. She was looking forward to finally going back to her home and family, to the simple quiet countryside, away from the noise and bustle of the hospital that she had been subjected to since her admittance over a year ago. Happily, she was preparing to go back home to a familiar environment.

It was not uncommon for people who had had surgical procedures to be in this medical ward. At the time there were no separate wards for patients recovering from surgery. The young woman to my left needed gall bladder surgery. She was a young mother of three who stayed only nine days to recuperate until her stitches were removed. Some people came and left, while others came and died.

I was sixteen years old when I arrived at the Royal Victoria Hospital, admitted with infectious hepatitis. Within minutes of my arrival, an eager young medical student from McGill University came and sat by my bed. This was the daily routine for student doctors. His horn-rimmed brown glasses sat on a very pimply face. He carried a note pad and was prepared with a series of questions. Although this young doctor was soft-spoken and polite, his appearance was less than inspiring for a young teenager in crisis. I really just wanted him to go and leave me alone.

Medical students would spend time at the hospital after their classes at the university. They would attempt to take case histories and establish some rapport with the patients both in the clinic and on the wards. This part of their apprenticeship was one of the required obligations of their medical education to eventually qualify them as doctors.

When it was my turn to be visited, I remember my strong sense of resentment towards these young students. I disliked and resented questions that never seemed to cease. These were the same questions which I had answered several times previously. I was irritable and tired, and I did not feel well. I just wanted to be left alone to sleep. I was exhausted from a prior sleepless night in the hectic environment of the emergency room. Soon after this young doctor left, another doctor and a group of interns slowly sauntered to my bedside. I could feel the blood in my veins surge with fire. I felt angry, annoyed, violated, and so very, very tired!

The curtains around the bed were drawn closed while an endocrinologist slowly examined me. When he had concluded his examination, the group took turns poking and probing my body. My skin was checked for colour and dryness, my eyelids were pulled down to check my eyeballs for jaundice and anemia, and my fingernails were pressed to see if the colour would return. I felt like a specimen under scrutiny underneath a giant microscope. In reality I was. My tolerance was very low and I was extremely upset. Finally after what seemed like a lifetime, the group of interns, satisfied with their findings, withdrew in a huddle at the end of the bed to confer. One of my problems, they decided, was that my abdomen was impacted. I was therefore given a combination of potent solutions to flush out my system.

Within a few minutes of the second treatment, I had to make a wild dash to that bathroom at the very end of the ward. Frightened and helpless, I sat in agony for what seemed to be an eternity. I was alone and did not know how to call for help. There was no call bell and my voice was very weak. The substances that I was administered gave me tremendous abdominal pain as I emptied my bowels, and my body went into physical shock. My muscles and fingers stiffened together and felt like wooden sticks. My body was so weak from all the abuse it had already suffered that day.

After waiting for a prolonged period of time, a patient who needed to use the facility finally found me and called in a nurse. I was taken back to my bed and left, for a short while at least, in peace.

By the time I was back in my bed it was already late in the afternoon. A nurse gave me a container of pills to take. To lessen the chances of vomiting, I had to swallow them without any liquid. This was immediately followed by two injections each consisting of two and a half c.c.'s of Gravol for nausea prevention.

It was now suppertime in the ward. The noisy rhythm and clatter of the trays being distributed from bed to bed only increased my throbbing headache. A tray of food, attractively presented, was placed on the table in front of me. I slowly picked up the lid covering the plate, peered at the tray, and fell back against my pillows. Weakened by the ordeal of the afternoon I had no appetite and I did not try to eat.

Drugged and in a sort of a semi-conscious state, I needed to close my eyes and try to sleep. A nurse, noticing that I had not touched my food, sat beside me and tried to feed me. Each morsel of food felt like I was swallowing hot coals. I was on fire from within. The pain was so excruciating that I started to scream and began vomiting blood. From then on I was kept on a bland diet and left to decide if and what I could eat. My first meal at the hospital proved to be a terrible nightmare.

Interns always accompanied doctors making their rounds. Like a slow swarm of white insects, they would go from patient to patient, drawing curtains around each bed as they proceeded. This was their daily routine, escorted by a senior doctor who would examine the patient and then let the interns take turns. For the interns this was a simple routine. This was a teaching hospital, one for which I was not so thrilled to donate my body or my illness.

It was intimidating having so many people scrutinizing and probing my body. After each examination, the swarm in white coats would go to the end of the bed to confer outside the still drawn curtain. Interns were then given the opportunity to comment about their findings and make suggestions about the treatment to follow. It was not uncommon for an intern to occasionally return to re-examine a patient before proceeding to the next one. This was one of many daily rituals for every patient in this ward. I despised these meetings!

Every ward had a clown. "Pip Squeak " was the nickname for a spry and happy eighty-nine-year-old, seventy-five pound, sweet-natured maiden lady. Every morning while struggling to don a dressing gown, her yellowing wavy hair in a half braid, she would perform a ritual dance by making a wild dash in the direction of the bathroom. As always she was unsuccessful at timing herself, leaving a foul smelling wet trail as she rushed along. Instead of embarrassment, her bubbly and positive outlook and good sense of humour was a daily inspiration for us all. This little woman was charming and cute.

Another patient was an elderly, grumpy and malcontent woman who continually complained about her constipation. Apparently being in the hospital was the cause of her terrible affliction. The hospital food was not as good as she thought it should be, and she felt the food was much better at her own home. According to her, the doctors were not attentive enough for her, the ward was much too draughty and cold, or it was too hot and stuffy. Every night she would demand of the nurses to have extra laxatives because the medication prescribed to her was not helping. Was "Pip Squeak " accidentally taking this miserable woman's laxatives?

Another young patient in this ward had spent most of her life in the care of nuns at a convent. She was a pretty young girl who had unfortunately been born without fingers. The nuns at the convent had taught her how to use her toes in place of fingers to accomplish simple daily tasks. Some of these tasks included washing, combing her hair, eating, and applying makeup, all of which she so competently achieved. With her upbeat and wonderful sense of humour, she possessed a quality that was needed to sustain life in her condition.

Plastic surgeons were attempting to build fingers from existing stubs on her hands. Each procedure was a process of grafting which extended the length of the stubs for her fingers. This series of surgeries was to continue until a desired outcome was achieved. With each grafting there was always some success. It did not matter if it would take a lifetime, for this positive young girl was prepared to wait an eternity if she must in order to possess normal hands.

Some patients were afflicted with the pain and discomfort of arthritis. A very kind and gentle doctor was trying to find a cure for, or at least a reduction to, the suffering of his patients. Every day he would see his patients, sit with them, and listen to their aches and complaints. He was interested in knowing whether the treatment being tried was helping in the relief of their pain. If not, he would suggest that maybe another method should be attempted. His presence in the ward had a calming effect on all the patients.

This kind doctor made each one of his patients feel that they were very important to him. He was their friend as well as their doctor. All of his patients liked and trusted him and felt comfortable in his presence. At least he was sincere. His patients were as anxious for him to succeed in his attempts to find a cure as he was in relieving them of their suffering. He had come from England and was only temporarily at this hospital. He was at the end of a required three-month term. Everyone was sorry to see him leave.

A NATO military doctor arrived at the Royal Victoria Hospital. He was mistrusted and feared by every patient with whom he had any contact. His stiff walk reflected his personality. He did not smile, he was brusque, and he seemed apathetic. People who feel ill need empathy and kindness. His manner did not render positively to any of the patients. Patients feared being in his presence. This military doctor was quite a contrast to his gentle, pleasant, and caring counterpart.

One of this military doctor's "victims" was a young mother of two small children who had endured four years in a marriage to a husband who was hardly ever home. Pregnant again, she was overworked, overstressed, and deprived of adult companionship. It was not surprising that she needed at least some rest and some adult stimulation. Understandably her main complaint was extreme fatigue.

Almost every afternoon during the week the doctor would wheel her out in her bed to one of the treatment rooms behind the nurse's station. Hours later a nurse would wheel her back to her room, sound asleep while yet "talking" in a stupor. The patients who were mobile would cluster around her bed, and have their amusement of the day eavesdropping and regaling in this unsuspecting woman's entire deep and dark secrets. The drug that was used would keep her unaware and mumbling until she awoke several hours later in the evening.

In the 1950's, television was not available in hospital wards. Few patients brought in a radio so that anything unusual, such as someone in the ward talking in their sleep, would be enough motivation to perk up one's interest. Patients returning from one of these treatments quickly achieved notoriety in the ward. Little did they know that they were the source of entertainment for that evening. This was better than the popular television program of the late 1950's, "Kraft Music Hall."

This frightening medical doctor seemed to choose his test subjects at random. I was terrified that he would get to me sooner or later. I pleaded with my mother to speak to the nurses so as not to allow this doctor to approach me. My mother did speak to the nurses but was told that they, the nurses, had no control over whom the doctors chose to treat. The nurses only followed instructions from the doctors. It was made quite clear that whatever the doctors were doing was in the best interest for the recovery of the patient.

This was the era prior to Universal Health Care in Canada. People without an insurance health plan had to pay their own hospital bills. Only those who were on welfare were exempt. Many of the patients admitted to this ward were welfare recipients. It was not a great surprise that some doctors felt that they had the right to try theories and unproven cures on patients, which at many times became curses to these people. There was no way to dispute any medical orders. Welfare patients could not sue doctors. The government was footing the medical payments so expenses and treatments were not an issue. Patients' complaints were unheeded. Was not everything being tried in the interest of getting patients well, even if the cure was worse than the disease?

Daily hospital visiting hours were from 2:00 until 4:00 p.m., and 7:00 to 8:00 p.m. in the evening. Two o'clock seemed to be the magical hour when most of the patients expecting visitors donned new characters. It was amazing how a swipe of lipstick, some rouge, a hair combing, and a change of nightgown transformed the ailing bodies into smiling beauties. This was quite in contrast to the mundane existence we experienced daily in the ward.

The visitors all seemed to swarm en masse like honeybees to a hive, dispersing to various bedsides along each side of the ward. Time spent with a patient varied. There was always some laughing, some crying, and lots of chatter. The ward was a lively place during these hours. The visitors created a sort of quiet chaos during the visiting hours, all of which was welcomed by the patients. This new energy broke up the monotony of an otherwise difficult day for patients. However it was probably very disruptive to the nursing staff, who still had to continue with the regular daily routine of fulfilling all the doctors' orders for each patient.

My relatives did come, but as time passed, the visitations became less frequent. Eventually my mother was my only visitor. Although I wanted and needed company, when people came I wanted them to leave. I was too weak to think, let alone try to have a conversation. It was a constant struggle trying to keep awake while being heavily sedated. I felt guilty for sleeping when visitors were present. If I tried to speak, the exertion would result in my being sick. This would make me totally dependent on the kidney basin beside my bed. It was repulsive watching some one continuously retching. It was embarrassing to let anyone see me in such a state. I was emotionally and physically drained. Anyone visiting would find it depressing and discouraging. It was understandable that visitors to my bedside dwindled and finally stopped coming.

Each patient was assigned to a specific doctor's service, which consisted of the head of a department, resident doctors, and interns. They would make the daily rounds together. After each patient was examined, this group would confer at the end of each bed, speaking in low voices. They would discuss whether or not there was improvement, what tests should be tried, whether the medication needed to be changed, and who was to be discharged that day.

At that time the average hospital duration was two weeks. That was apparently enough time for prescribed tests and medication to heal an ailment. After being discharged, a patient was either seen by a private physician or at a clinic. If problems persisted, patients could be seen again at the hospital clinic.

The head of the gastroenterology department confirmed that I had hepatitis. Although I had become subdued and passive to being examined by so many doctors, it still bothered me after so many weeks. Each time I was examined I felt stripped of my dignity. After each examination the group of student doctors would gather at the end of my bed to decide on the day's strategy against my illness.

Due to continuous vomiting I was also being treated for anorexia nervosa. Therefore, prior to every meal, I was given three injections to aid in trying to solve this vomiting problem. Two shots were Gravol to try to stop the retching, and the other shot was insulin to stimulate my appetite. These injections were followed twenty minutes later by a large glass of glucose in orange juice for me to drink, and more pills for me to swallow.

Horrible vitamin shots were injected into me every other day. The burning sting of these injections lingered for quite some time. These shots were so painful that I would cry. Potassium chloride was also added to the regular daily intravenous feedings of dextrose and water. Being hooked to an I.V. and being attacked with injections several times a day was not conducive to a comfortable or pleasant healing process.

From early morning until lights out at 9:00 p.m., the ward was in perpetual activity. Mid-morning noises included the pushing of patients in their metal beds to the centre of the room by the housekeeping staff. It was at this time that they washed each individual bed area. Swishing heavy mops, and clanging metal buckets oozing of disinfectant, they cleaned and moved about to a mechanical rhythm until the entire floor area was washed. The cleaning staff contributed to the activity and action, dusting, sweeping, mopping, and disinfecting around each bed as they waltzed through their regular chores.

Every day the orderlies and attendants would take patients requiring x-rays or surgery to various medical departments. Nurses and technicians were kept busy changing bed linen, taking blood, doing cardiograms, and attending to patients' needs. A nurse with medication, or a technician filling out a test request, would interrupt anyone whether they were trying to nap, or had visitors. The daily routine of the staff measuring temperatures, checking blood pressure, taking blood samples, adjusting intravenous apparatus, replacing used bedpans, or performing regular daily rounds was never interrupted.

Daily blood tests and intravenous feedings caused my veins to become fragile and in turn led to the extreme agony of ceaseless pain in my arms. I cringed and dreaded each needle attack. I wondered if the needles and syringes back in the `1950's might have been fragile because of constant re-use and sterilization. It was a regular event for them to break. If a syringe was damaged during a blood taking process, which was a regular occurrence, another syringe was attached. I was often left bleeding, the needle minus the syringe stuck in my arm. I remember quite vividly that even when pressure was applied it was not enough to inhibit the leakage of blood from the syringe. Whenever this happened my bed would be drenched in blood. This meant that the bedding had to be changed yet again. It was a process I terribly despised because any attempt to get out of and into bed again was very exhausting for me in my weakened condition.

Disposable needles and syringes, as we know them today, were not yet available or even commonly used. Blocked syringes and blunt needles were a common occurrence. Being a victim of needle abuse, I felt like a pincushion.

Lumping and bruising was the result of the daily intra-muscular shots. My arms began to look like they were tattooed from all the blood tests and intravenous feedings. I looked terrible and felt embarrassed by my battle scars.

Every day was the same! I was living a nightmare and I was constantly under scrutiny by the doctors and the interns at the hospital. The daily tests I had to undergo, the various medications, and the variety of diets that the doctors put me on did not help to improve my condition. It seemed only to worsen my state of being. I felt like I was dying.

The gurgling, rasping, and grinding sounds of a suction machine, the life support for a very ill patient, was the common background music in the horror film that I felt I was living. These were familiar sounds in the ward. Almost daily, a new patient would replace a person who was discharged, or one who had died the previous night. I felt like the living dead. Every night I found myself wondering if this was to be my last night on earth. I was so afraid of dying. I felt helpless and unable to will myself to get better.

One day I experienced a major reality check. I realized that I had changed. Who was that ghost staring back at me from the mirror? Never before had I seen such a chalky white person. The white bed sheets had more colour than I did. It was not a wonder that some of my friends would burst into tears when they came to visit because this really was not me! They were frightened, and I think they believed I was dying. Being several pounds lighter, my olive complexion having turned white, I did not recognize myself either. My image must have appalled them.

It must have been quite distressing to see a breathing corpse. That was my state of being. I had become a carcass waiting for death! Not so long ago, I was a healthy and vivacious young person with colour in my cheeks and a clear complexion. I had rapidly digressed to a near skeletal appearance, with a sickly pallour to my skin because of a dramatic loss of skin pigment.

It was obvious to me that the reason for the rare visitations from friends and family was due in large part to the distress of seeing me as I had become. It was aggravating for me to see myself in this state, the victim who nobody wanted to see. My condition was pulling me down into a hopeless abyss. How could doctors place people in such conditions for their own advancement?

I was angry and envious of everyone, especially of all those people who were effortlessly talking, walking, laughing, and going about their lives in a regular manner. I would lie in bed day after day in great discomfort and pain. As I became weaker I continually felt that I was leading a terrible existence. I was angry! I felt sorry for myself. Simply making what would normally be considered an effortless and automatic gesture was an ordeal that always triggered a vomiting attack. My mother was being torn apart watching me deteriorate. She felt helpless.

I was being kept in a drugged state. Getting out of bed was another horrible and traumatic experience. Taking a step was a struggle because I had so little energy, and exerting physical effort of any kind would cause me to have a blackout. I would experience a terrifying spinning sensation, visualize a temporary blindness or black dots behind my eyes, a pins and needles sensation throughout my body, and a buzzing in my ears. Although these occurrences lasted only for a few seconds, they lasted long enough to upset me. Blindly groping for the nearest bed, I would scream and cry for help. This again promoted the vomiting, so I always carried a kidney basin for security. This was the result of continuously being kept in a drugged state.

Except for a few relatives every now and then, visitors eventually stopped coming. One of my aunts believed that the incident when my mother's ex-boyfriend had tried to stab me probably caused my illness. During one of her visits she decided to tell a doctor about the attack. Even though this attack had happened several months prior to my illness, this tidbit of gossip delighted the doctors. Now they had a different theory about what was causing my hepatitis.

At the time of my initial diagnosis in the 1950's, there were several confirmed cases of hepatitis on the North Shore of Montreal. It did not seem to matter that I could have contracted this disease by drinking contaminated water. Maybe it was a convenient excuse for trying further tests. No one considered the large quantity of Largactil, a known aggravator of hepatitis, that I was ingesting daily.

2   LARGACTIL – one of the strongest and most efficient tranquillizers ever invented is Largactil. – It works directly on the thalamus, depressing activity in the part of the brain which regulates and stimulates physical and emotional responses. It has a rapid and decisive calming effect on people who are over-excited or violent, and is one of the most useful additions to the pharmacopoeia for mental patients. But caution is required because of its side-effects, which have on rare occasions proved lethal. – the thalamus also controls body temperature. Largactil users who complain of cold are not merely being oversensitive to the weather. Their medication can actually cause their bodies to fall to subnormal temperatures with dangerous – and can be fatal. Another side-effect – very rare – a lack of white blood cells. (C.P. 46)

Sodium Amytal, Largactil, Stelazine, Trofinal, and Trilafon were among many of the daily regime of pills I was given to swallow. If I vomited I was given more to take. These were all ingested without   liquid   and   caused   me   tremendous heartburn. The thought of eating, swallowing, or even talking, would fill my throat with blood. I would scream and cry. The severe burning pain was so unbearable that the mere thought of food had become a terrible punishment. I could not endure so much physical pain.

My condition was rapidly worsening and my depression was deepening. This was a result of the large quantity of medication, the illness itself, or both. For weeks I was in a semi-conscience state. Rumour on the ward had it that I was dying. Actually, I was dying! I could feel myself slowly slipping away and could not help myself. I had lost the will to live because life was too painful.

Was I dreaming? Someone was gently stroking my hair. A soft voice was telling me to fight and live, that I was too young to die, and I had too many dreams to fulfill. Did I really want to die? It was an empathetic doctor doing his nightly round before signing out. He gave me the incentive to fight. It was a struggle and being so groggy made my every effort much more difficult. This man was considerate, kind, gentle, caring, and well liked by both the staff and the patients.

With this doctor's encouragement, I slowly began to recuperate. I tried to read but found it impossible, as my concentration was very limited. Art interested me. Someone had brought me a "paint by number" kit and soon painting became a daily afternoon activity. I had really begun to recuperate, but not soon enough to be discharged before coming into the clutches of the dreaded NATO military doctor!

Many patients had the misfortune of being summoned by this short and stocky middle-aged man. He was feared. His rigid walk, stern wooden expressionless face, and short military haircut made him imposing. He would not or could not smile, and he never answered any questions. Indeed, he was neither a friendly nor a charming fellow.

The tray which he habitually carried with him whenever he was in this ward contained vials, plastic tubing, large elastic bands, syringes, needles, and swabs. His approach was that of a person preparing a victim for torture. At that moment, I wanted to die rather than let him touch me. Who knew what tortures he had planned each day to satisfy his sadistic ego? His halitosis was severe, which of course did not add to his charisma or charm. What would happen to me after I was wheeled out of the ward with him?

The sodium amytal that he injected into my vein put me out immediately. Surprisingly it was actually a beautiful feeling, just gently slipping into oblivion. Whatever transpired during those sessions, and there were many of them, I shall never know. I always awoke in the ward several hours later. This was the ritual. My questions to him were never answered and the only information that I was given was that everything being done was to help me get better. Was I now the new entertainment in the ward?

It was known that experiments testing sodium amytal, known as truth serum, were being done on unsuspecting patients.

3   AMYTAL – a barbiturate with a hypnotic effect." (p. 13)

This research was based on the effects of brainwashing of soldiers during the Korean War. It was rumoured by patients in the ward that doctors were trying to find methods that the enemy used to drive the P.O.W's to breakdown, and methods that were used on military personnel.

#4 Drugs – "William Sargant, a British psychiatrist who had his first taste of therapeutic success with war neurotics, was quick to realize that "World War II provided medicine with rare opportunities for studying the breakdown of normal persons subjected to intense stress," and that early in the war "the value of certain drugs had become obvious in helping patients to discharge their pent-up emotions about the terrifying experiences which had caused their mental breakdown." "The goal that soon intrigued the secret warriors, of course, was how to reap the naked truth, the real dope, the pearl of hidden information, from among the personal debris." "The methods used to near psychic breaks on the beaches of Normandy might hold the key to perfect interrogation." (W. p.39)

During the five to six weeks that I spent in this ward, my liver and abdomen were subjected to daily probing by doctors, interns, and medical students. A medical student could pick up a patient file and stroll over any time to learn whatever he needed and wanted to know. Blood tests, x-rays, and stool and urine analysis were part of the daily routine. At least some of these tests were harmless and painless.

Proctoscopes and gastroscopes at that time required general anesthesia. These were scopes inserted deep into the body. Scrapings of the esophagus, stomach, and intestines were taken for analysis. These tests were used to check for any possible diseases known at that time. Any conceivable test invented was tried. Dignity was a luxury rather than a patient's right, so that anyone wearing a white coat had license and authority to abuse patients in the name of medicine.

Patients were specimens to be analyzed like microbes underneath a microscope. However, I did have an enlarged liver and spleen, possibly due to the daily probing by the medical squad. My stomach and bowels seemed healthy although I suffered the discomfort of constipation and continuous vomiting. As for my kidneys and urinary tract, passing sand and blood was not unusual. My blood chemistry was totally out of sync, and needless to say I was severely anemic. I had a very pathetic body, I was continuously crying. Three days after being discharged from the RVH I was admitted to the Allan Memorial Institute (AMI) with severe depression.

CHAPTER 5

CHAMBER OF HORROR

5   Ravenscrag – The Allan Memorial Institute – AMI. [It was] T – shaped and three storeys high, out at the back of the building. (W.p.10)

This hulking gray stone mansion was situated on the south side of Mount Royal Mountain. Ravensgrag, referred to as "The Mansion," and known as the Allan Memorial Institute, (AMI), was the psychiatric ward of the Royal Victoria Hospital. This was a separate building away from the main complex. Although this gray stone building was situated on a slope on the south side of Mount Royal Mountain, it was partially hidden by a forest of trees that surrounded the well-manicured and enormous grounds.   Overlooking the city skyline and the St. Lawrence River, it yielded a magnificent vista.   There had been a recent addition to the back of this mansion adding another ward to the second floor. A hallway attaching the new building to "The Mansion" in the shape of a "T" separated these wards.

Allan Memorial Institute "Ravenscrag"
Virtual McGill
Allan Memorial Institute -- McGill Archives

In 1863, Sir Hugh Allan, the Scottish founder and president of the Allan Lines Shipping Company, commissioned Victor Roy and John Hopkins to construct a house that reflected his wealth and power. This Italianate, villa-style mansion was named Ravenscrag after a Scottish castle and was located at the top of McTavish Street with an imposing view over the entire city. The house, which is divided into many wings, had an asymmetric facade dominated by a large, solid tower which dominates the main entrance. The thirty-four room interior featured a different architectural style in each room. The entrance hall and dining room had Italian themes, the ballroom was French, and the oak-paneled library with ornate furniture was distinctly Victorian. Since the Allans were interested in horses, the fourteen acre estate possessed one of the finest stables on the Square Mile, the entrance of which was marked by a sculpted horse's head.

After Sir Hugh Allan died in 1882, his son and daughter-in-law, Sir Montagu and Marguerite, respectively, inherited Ravenscrag. They enlarged the house, redecorated in a more elegant and lavish style, employed several live-in servants, and filled the stable with prize thoroughbreds at the request of Sir Montagu, the president of the Jockey Club. After Sir Montagu's death, Lady Allan gave Ravenscrag to the Royal Victoria Hospital in 1940. It was renamed the Allan Memorial Institute in 1943. To serve the present needs as a psychiatric hospital and research institute, the interior of the building has been altered and many additions have been made to the exterior.

Built 1863

Architects - Victor Roy and John Hopkins

Donor - Allan family

Current use - Psychiatric research institute

"Ravenscrag" (1902)
-- Notman Archive (McCord Museum)

Stable & Coachhouse (1903)
Notman Archive (McCord Museum)

Additional Pictures of the Allan Memorial
Institute, "Ravenscrag"
View from the East (1903) -- Notman Archive
(McCord Museum)
Sitting room (1902) -- Notman Archive (McCord
Museum)
Allan Memorial Institute -- Instructional
Communications Centre\

Lady Allan's drawing room (1911)
Notman Archive (McCord Museum)

Lounge & hall (1902)
Notman Archive (McCord Museum)

When I was admitted, beds were not available at the Allan Memorial Institute, so I became a day patient. A day patient was equally as ill as a full time patient, except that the day patient attended the hospital on a daily basis rather than being admitted full time. It was more like attending school or going to work every day. Treatment and medication were administered according to the gravity of the illness and at the discretion of the assigned doctor. It was possible therefore that a full-time patient could be receiving less medication and fewer treatments than a day patient.

An AMI day patient arrived Monday through Friday at 8:30 in the morning and left at 4:30 in the afternoon. Fresh doughnuts and the aroma of hot beverages of coffee, tea, and chocolate wafted through the ward as the various patients slowly trekked in each morning. At lunchtime a hot meal of meat, fish, or eggs with vegetables, dessert, and a beverage was served. The needs of patients requiring specific diets were respected. Sandwiches of liverwurst or peanut butter and jam, tea, coffee, and juice were prepared and available at two-thirty in the afternoon. Anyone with a healthy appetite could not possibly go home hungry.

Electro-shock (ECTs) and other treatments were rendered each day to those who required them, and daily medication was issued at the prescribed time to each patient. Prior to our departure at 4:30 p.m., our evening medication was distributed to each one of us in a little envelope to take at home. Insulin-shock therapy was administered on weekends only. Patients requiring this therapy stayed over the weekend. Insulin-shock treatment was painful and dangerous. These patients in particular required special supervision and had to be continuously monitored until they awoke.

Chemical Convulsions and Schizophrenia

The Insulin Shock Therapy

Insulin coma required five to nine hours of hospitalization and close follow-up, but it was easily controlled and stopped with injections of glucose or adrenalin, when needed. Metrazol was stronger and more difficult to control. Insulin therapy caused few side effects, while metrazol convulsions were so severe that they caused spine fractures in 42 % of the patients!

www.epub.org.br/cm/n04/historia/shock_i.htm

On the second floor of the new addition, there were doctors' offices, laboratories, and extra rooms for various uses. These were on either side of the wide hallway. The day ward was downstairs. Even with this new addition, there was still only the one kitchen for all the patients in each of the wards. It was situated upstairs in the old part of the building behind the nursing station.

The day ward on the main floor had a staff library, seminar rooms, a large art room, a little coffee shop, a hairdressing salon, a kitchen for the day patients, and more doctors' offices. Coming in from the outside and not knowing that this was a hospital, one could almost mistake these premises for a small elaborate private hotel.

6   The establishment of the pioneering Day Hospital at the Allan in 1946 was typical of Cameron. Strapped for space and for beds, and longing in expansionary fashion to draw in more

patients Cameron began to wonder whether a bed was at all necessary for treatment in the first place. (C.p.115)

The solution was a department that mimicked working hours: patients would check in from 8:30 a.m. to 4:30 p.m., go home at nights, and have their weekends off. If they were ongoing either ECT or insulin treatment, that could be done during the day too," by borrowing a bed from a full time patient." (C. p.115)

What is a psychiatric ward? Are people walking around like zombies or screaming hysterically? Are the patients in straight jackets and kept in padded cells? I really did not know what to expect and I was frightened of what would happen to me.

One of the psychiatrists assigned to me at the AMI was not too pleased to learn that I had recently been discharged from the medical ward. After a preliminary examination he felt that I was still ill with hepatitis. The BSP, a blood test whereby dye was injected into my vein and blood drawn a half-hour later, proved that my liver was still not functioning properly. The doctor thought that I should still be in the medical ward. Thinking about it now, I presume the absorption of the dye would show the level of bilirubin, which determined if the liver was functioning properly or not. At that time my liver was still enlarged and tender to the touch, and my skin was still dry and itchy. I was extremely depressed. I wept constantly and for no apparent reason.

The "Torture Chamber," or EEG Lab, was in the attic. The "Dungeon" was in the old basement of the main building where psychological and I.Q. testing was done. Within my first week I was stripped of whatever dignity I might have still possessed, literally from the top to the bottom, from the attic to the basement.

The psychological and I.Q. testing proceeded in stages and over many days. Working through the complete battery of tests left me feeling degraded and belittled. The psychologists were also doing additional research, and although they may have been following standard guidelines throughout the tests, I am sure that some of the games and questions were intended for children of pre-school age. I did what was asked. I responded to the questions and was relieved when it was finally over. Throughout the whole time I kept on weeping.

The EEG laboratory was quite different. The attic was small and all the available space was filled either by a bed, lights, or some type of machinery. There were two technicians. One very friendly and talkative technician told me that she would be using a painless procedure to record my brainwaves. I had nothing to be afraid of though it would take some time. I was not prepared for what was about to happen.

The indignity of allowing my head to be measured and then having my head dabbed with a red marker was embarrassing. Pieces of hair were snipped from twenty-one strategic spots on my head, cold jelly cement was slathered on, and finally electrical probes were cemented where the hair had been snipped away. This I felt was going too far. I wanted to scream and run away. I was incredibly angry and I could not stop crying. With all the probes sticking out of my head, I must have looked like Medusa, the mythological woman whose head was covered in snakes. With all the probes sticking to my head I was carefully helped onto the bed. Little did I know what was to follow!

Laying on the bed with the probes sticking out all over my head was intimidating even though it was actually quite painless, and really not that terrible. The probe wires were attached to a machine that the technician was monitoring. I thought that the whole procedure would soon be over. I waited impatiently for all of this to end. I just could not endure the discomfort and indignity any longer. I had little patience and I wanted to leave. If I thought this to be torture, I was definitely not prepared for my next treat.

Long thin probes resembling two large knitting needles were inserted deep into each nostril. I was assured that the ends were anesthetized and should not hurt, but it was still painful. I was told that these probes would record waves from beneath my brain.

Strobe lights were then placed directly over my face. At first the lights flashed slowly but then began progressively speeding up. I was ordered to keep my eyes open. I could not take this any longer. With all that apparatus attached to me, I was not capable of pulling any of it off without hurting myself. Inside I was screaming. Finally the ordeal was over, and I shamefully left, hiding my head in a scarf.

My once clean and shining hair now stood up stiffly from all that caked on sticky substance. All the red spots that were dabbed onto my head were still visible, even though the technician really did try to clean them. Months later, my head showed shoots of hair protruding like crabgrass in a garden patch where the hair had once been snipped.

The EEG took several hours. I had spent the whole day confined, agitated, and crying. It was finally time to collect my medication and leave the hospital. Having wrapped a heavy scarf over my pathetic looking hair to try and hide my newly acquired battle scars, it was a relief to finally go home for the night.

The everyday smells of coffee, tea, hot cocoa, and doughnuts greeted patients each morning as they arrived. Morning medication was administered and then patients began their daily routine of complaints. "What a terrible night." "My wife and children are driving me crazy." "I can't help it if I'm sick". And on and on.

Patients went for occupational therapy or art, sat and smoked, or had their electro-shock treatments. Some would wander about aimlessly or sit and complain about headaches and the fact that they were losing their memory. The odd patient would take advantage of the wonderful selection of books in the library to read, play cards, or try to play the piano in the activity room. Each day was a repeat of the previous one, with only a slight change when different patients rotated for their treatments.

The library was my refuge, not so much as a place to read, but to rest my battered body in a deep and comfortable armchair. The large windows brightened up the room, and if the sun was shinning, it was comforting to soak up the bright warm soothing rays. The library also served as a refuge for many other patients. Although only a few people read, others quietly played board games or cards, or sat motionless as I did. A few even mingled together and conducted meaningless conversations. It did not matter or bother anyone that I was always weeping, because everyone here also had a problem. The library was the most comfortable place to sit, rest, and wait, until it was time to leave for home.

Sessions with doctors in the day hospital continued at regular intervals of two or three times a week. Many were not pleased and would have preferred much more allotted time with their doctor, while others detested any contact with any of the staff. Psychotherapy was painless but emotionally it could be tormenting. Many patients would have preferred to be left alone without having to undergo any treatment.

Occupational therapy was encouraged, but few people made use of the wonderful facilities that were available for all of the patients at the AMI. Water and oil painting, charcoal, ceramics, pottery, cooking, sewing, and basket weaving were always available and accompanied by very capable instructors and therapists.

Some patients were forced to attend occupational therapy sessions, and would sit solemnly for the duration rather than try to participate or get involved. But eventually, they too would yield to the ambiance of the room and produce wonderful pieces of art. Some sewed an apron, skirt, or blouse, while others baked cakes and cookies. Everything that was created was unfortunately a grim souvenir of time spent within these walls.

Basket weaving did not interest me. The clay of the pottery felt cold and I did not like that cold feeling. Eventually over a period of time I did manage to sew myself a skirt from one of the many patterns that was available. I also enjoyed baking, and the warmth of the kitchen was enticing because I was always cold. It was pleasant working in a warm environment.

My accomplishment in the kitchen was a perfect spice cake that I offered to my doctor. I did not want to take it home. First it was a grim reminder of how and where I now spent my days. Furthermore I did not like spice cake. The picture of the cake looked pretty and all the ingredients for the recipe were available so I tried making it. I have not made a spice cake since.

Doors at the AMI were not locked. Although it was easy to come and go, most of us had emotional restraints that kept us from escaping or just walking away. Patients wandered everywhere in and around the premises and even to the downtown core. Some knew where they were going, some went for a stroll downtown, and some would get lost. Most patients wanted to leave and to get away from the hospital, doctors, and treatments. But we all kept coming back daily.

Smoke always permeated the wide hallway to the entrance that was off the vestibule. This area was lined with chairs, allowing several patients at a time to sit and enjoy their favourite past-time of resting idly, smoking, and staring into space for hours on end. So many were smoking that the smoke sat over them like a thick heavy cloud.

I did not smoke and could not stand the smell. Although we were all medicated to some degree, I would look at these people and wonder, "*What did we have in common?*" They all looked so pathetic that I could not relate to them. A conversation of any depth was almost impossible, and would invariably be monotone and centered on our personal ills. I did not feel as they did because I was aware of my surroundings. I was capable of recognizing people. I accepted that my concentration level was minimal, my body movements were sluggish, and I was constantly weeping. Yet I could not just sit and stare blankly into space for hours on end like the majority of these patients, because my sluggish mind was still active and I was continually thinking.

The majority of the patient population was undergoing a series of electro-shock treatments. Many complained continuously of having severe headaches, or that they suffered severe memory loss and were making every effort to remember things. Others were passing the time in the canteen. They were also smoking, sitting and eating sandwiches, cake, or chocolate bars, drinking coffee or tea, and conjuring big plans about "When I get out of here."

We were encouraged to use board games such as snakes and ladders or monopoly, playing cards, books, puzzles, and even a decent piano which were available for our use. The daily meals were hot, tasty, and abundant. The specific diets required for various patients were respected, and food was always attractively served to be enjoyed by most of us. The motto must have been, "Feed the body, heal the mind." And then came more medication.

Group therapy was not as popular as the weekly travelogues. Although these weekly sessions were compulsory, people floated in and out of the room as they pleased. Grunting, muttering, mumbling, complaining, crying, or laughing hysterically was typical in these therapy sessions. Because of the heavy medication, some people had the shakes. It was impossible to sit at a table if one was shaking, because one's knees would knock over the table, scattering anything on it to the floor. Patients suffering from the shakes could not sit for any prolonged period of time. Everyone here lived in a fog, the mind separated from the body.

The doctor heading the group therapy would try to encourage a discussion for some feedback and response to stimulate our brain function. With a cocktail of coloured pills metered to the maximum to each patient, so numerous it was sometimes beyond our ability to cope with the sheer number, it was a wonder that we could even stand. The duration of these sessions were approximately one hour and very few patients remained to the end.

Four thirty was the hour of freedom, the long awaited moment. It was finally the end of the day and time to fly the coop. The nursing station would fill to capacity in almost an instant. Like children waiting for loot bags at the end of a party, everyone queued outside the nursing station anxious to receive the precious envelope of medication. Each envelope had enough medication until 8:00 the following morning.

This was the daily routine until the long awaited weekend. Then, like an army of ants, everyone rushed down the steep driveway, quickly being absorbed into the general flow of people hurrying home at rush hour. By four thirty-five the main floor of the AMI was empty, all the day patients nowhere to be seen. The only activity was that of the occasional "out" patient with an appointment to see a doctor.

CHAPTER 6

OBLIVION

Peel Street, starting at the bottom of the AMI at Pine St. until it reaches Sherbrooke St., is on an extremely steep hill. During the cold winter days in Montreal, when snow would freeze on the sidewalks, it became very treacherous for pedestrians to walk down the hill unless the sidewalks had been salted or sanded. Any attempt to walk down the hill without slipping and falling presented a major challenge. Many patients would leave the hospital together in small groups to go down to the bus stop. Huddling in small groups and holding on to each other, lessened the chance of sliding and falling down into oncoming cars. Leaving together also made us an instant social unit. Finally assimilating with passengers on a bus loaded with other people heading home after a long day at work helped us to blend in as regular people. The stigma of being in a mental institution was forgotten for a short while when mingling in with the general populace.

One afternoon, on such a snowy day, two of us left the hospital a short time later than the other patients, so we went down the slippery hill together. I was accompanying a patient afflicted with epilepsy. Suddenly she realized she was about to experience a seizure.

I had never before seen anyone having such an attack, and I was panic-stricken. Traffic was at its busiest and the falling snow made visibility poor. This poor woman had her seizure on the sidewalk and was slipping down helplessly. I was terrified that she would slip into the oncoming traffic and I did not know what to do. Frightened and weak, I tried to grab hold of a fence railing that was in front of one of the buildings. I tried frantically to keep her from slipping down to the intersection by grabbing her, and holding onto a fence at the same time. After her seizure was over, which seemed to go on forever, the weak, shaken, and slightly dazed woman slowly pulled herself up onto the metal fence. We continued on our way. We finally got onto a bus to go home. Still weak, she continued on as though nothing had happened. I, however, was still very shaken by the experience of seeing someone so helpless. I realized that she could have easily been killed had I not been there to keep her from slipping into harm's way.

About a week after being admitted to the Allan Memorial I was summoned to a seminar room. A senior member of the medical staff at that time was briefing a group of young medical students. My presence there was for the benefit of all those young potential doctors who were now entering the new and ever mysterious world of psychiatry. Each student had a copy of my medical history. Now was the chance for them to relate the written word to the front line of fieldwork.

A different method of treatment, and what medication would or would not be appropriate towards my recovery, was being discussed during the seminar. This ordeal lasted at least one hour. All the while I sat like a motionless zombie on a very uncomfortable wooden chair. I sat at the end of a long table while their eyes seemed to pierce through me. My depression was deep and my body was weak. How could these young, innocent, and naïve scholars, who were barely older than I, know how it felt to be so ill? How could they possibly consider themselves knowledgeable enough to try to cure the ills of the mind? What gave them the right to think that they knew how I felt?

Their questions were intimidating. Of course I knew what day it was. My depression did not affect my memory. I knew the date and also the month. I knew that I was a patient at the Allan and I remembered my name and my age, but most importantly I knew how I felt. Could this seminar shed some light on an appropriate treatment for my recovery? Or maybe after this session, my record would be filed and returned back to the shelf to collect dust.

I soon began to surmise that one of the treatments given daily to most of the patients at the AMI was electro-shock therapy. This was a constant worry to me. I was concerned for my own mental health. I realized the absurdity of my thoughts: this was a mental institute and I worried about my sanity!

Most ECT patients suffered memory loss and severe headaches, and seemed to be rendered dysfunctional after the treatments. I did not want to become like them. This was a great fear for me and I spoke of it often to my doctor. One particular doctor assured me that I was not in need of shock therapy and that he would "protect" me. From whom or what, he did not say.

My therapy sessions were three times a week. With his feet on the desk, leaning back on his chair, the psychiatrist would question me about my dreams. He was especially anxious about the dreams in every detail, and felt that I did not convey well enough that I had big problems. I should be complaining more. If every normal teenager in Canada had major problems, then why should I as a teenager not have problems?

I knew that I had problems, but his expectations were that mine should be insurmountable and that I should be constantly complaining about them. After the hour was over I would leave, not having resolved how I felt, and knowing that the following session would be a repeat of the last.

What deep and dark secrets were I expected to divulge? Throughout my life, from early childhood at home with an extended family, the Children's Home when I was six years old, and four years in

Summerhill House until I was fifteen, I had led a supervised, scrutinized, sheltered, and controlled existence. It would have been impossible for me to accumulate any secrets living within such environments. Each session with the doctor seemed to be a repeat of the previous one. With lethargy, crying, and vomiting as my complaints, why should I want more problems? A handful of different tranquilizers and barbiturates several times a day kept me quite sedated.

Largactal was always a large part of my four times a day drug cocktail. I could not possibly have a problem. I was kept in a sort of continuous mild oblivion. My mind was in a suspended state floating off on its own, not quite connected to my body. I could not think and do, although I still had the sense of right and wrong. But I was controlled by the drugs and like an obedient child, did as I was told.

Nitrous oxide, or laughing gas, to me was not a laughing matter! This was the next phase of my treatment. It was very simple. Three times a week I would be told to arrive at the hospital without having had any food or drink. I guess the reasons are similar to those used for general anesthesia. The gas had to be administered on an empty stomach to avoid possible complications, such as vomiting and choking. It was also obligatory for a nurse to be present each time the gas was being administered, and until I revived. My therapy sessions had changed. They now took place in this same room instead of the doctor's office, where I had previously had gas-free psychoanalysis. Now the doctor put me to sleep first, and then we communicated.

It was a simple procedure. The doctor placed a mask over my nose and mouth. Slowly I would drift into a spiraling abyss. Each time I had the feeling that I was a minute molecule, spinning faster and faster into a never-ending whirlpool. Was this the feeling of dying? Would I awake again, or would I keep on spinning forever? It was not a good feeling! I never knew how long I would be kept in this unconscious state.

A gentle tapping on my cheeks would always bring me back. What followed next were the ritual questions. What did I dream about? How long did I think each dream lasted? How long did I think that I was unconscious? The psychiatrist was obsessed with asking me the same questions at the conclusion of each procedure.

Finally one dream that was particularly focused upon had something to do with a moving train. The psychiatrist, a scholar of Dr. Sigmund Freud, thought that it could be related to sex. Freud considered movement in dreams to represent sex. After each session I was concerned about my thoughts of dying while under the influence of the nitrous oxide. I wondered whether this unnatural feeling would go on forever. To me, the moving train was just a dream, not frightening, not a nightmare, and not something that I felt was of any importance.

At that time occupational therapy was still too strenuous for me, but I started to sit in the art room and listen to the classical music that was constantly being played. The art therapist favoured the German composer Wagner, but she would also play selections of other classical composers. I was still extremely depressed, but the music seemed to ease a deep void that I felt. My attention span was still minimal, but the music was very soothing, and eventually I was encouraged to try doing some art while I was there.

Most patients in the art room did not seem affected by the music. Some sat in a catatonic state, stone-faced, oblivious to the sounds and their surroundings. Some were so heavily sedated they needed help coming to and leaving the room, and even had to be helped to do finger painting. I do not know if these people ever recovered. It was very sad to see a person active one day and in a vegetative state the next.

My wandering around the hospital and crying did not upset anyone. All the patients were dysfunctional in one way or another and living in their own spaces. We did not pay any attention to each other. Some patients complained about having lost their memories. They had blank expressions as they wandered about or just sat staring dumbly into space. These patients always occupied all the chairs in the hallway close to the front entrance. Smoking all day seemed to be the only function that they could perform or had any interest in doing.

Pottery was not interesting to me, nor were cooking or sewing. These activities were in the stables outside the east side of the main building. One section was reserved for clay and ceramics, and another section for basket weaving, sewing, and cooking. It was winter and too cold to walk even short distances. Going over to the stables also meant putting on a coat and hat and pulling boots on over our shoes. This in itself was a major chore.

Weakness and depression plagued me. Reading had been one of my favourite passions. At one time I could concentrate and read several books in a month. Now this was an impossible task. Would I ever get well? My body was not well and probably my extreme weakness kept me weeping. My mind was not confused and I did not get things mixed up. Was I actually mentally ill? There seemed to be no end or change in my state of health. One week rolled into another and then another. Where was my rainbow?

Medically trained blood technicians whom I referred to as "vampires" sought victims for blood samples. They were always waiting for each patient as they arrived every Monday morning. This was when everyone had his or her compulsory blood test of the week.

Monday was the most exciting day of the week and much more hectic than the other days. Most patients had had a terrible weekend. They complained either because their families could not cope with their mood or mood changes, or because some did not take their medication. Others took their weekend medication supply all at once on arriving home on Friday and then had to be rushed to the emergency at the RVH. A few were continuously attempting to commit suicide. Others mixed drugs and alcohol.

Monday also seemed to be the preferred day for processing the ECT patients who pathetically objected, pleaded, cried, and tried to hide, but to no avail. The doctor was God and everyone obeyed. Needless to say, Monday was the least popular day of the week for everyone.

It was already six weeks since my admission to the AMI. My depression was slowly diminishing. I was no longer walking around continuously crying, but

I was still vomiting and feeling tremendous pain in my liver. My pallour was not exactly a pretty pink or even peachy, but was rather somewhat yellow. Therefore it was not surprising that I once again was admitted with hepatitis to the medical ward at the Royal Victoria Hospital.

CHAPTER 7

WELCOME BACK

Blue, turquoise, gray, and pink were some of the rainbow colours of the pills that awaited me as I was wheeled back into the ward. Stelazine and Largactil were also among this lot. I was groggy and quite passive, and only wanted to sleep. I became aware of a cheerful nurse approached me. She was carrying two syringes, each filled with 2.5 c.c's of Gravol.

I asked her why I needed the Gravol. I told her that I felt very groggy and did not think that I could cope with more drugs. If my body was already so saturated with drugs so that I was made to feel ill, why did I need more? My protesting was useless and the nurse gave me the two shots. Drug oblivion overcame me and I went to sleep. I actually felt very nauseous when over-drugged. I was uncomfortable and recognized when my body had had enough.

This time I was admitted to the care of yet another doctor, along with a resident doctor under his guidance. Each doctor had a preference to certain drugs and the resident seemed fascinated by the colour blue. He always prescribed Stelazine. These pills were small, round, and a beautiful azure blue.

Drug slumber was not always wonderful. No sooner had I fallen asleep after being medicated than I was abruptly shaken awake. An orderly was trying to rouse me. He had a requisition form for me to have x-rays. This was impossible! Weak, lethargic, half sleeping, and feeling terribly ill, why would they not let me sleep? The orderly helped me with my dressing gown, sat me in the wheelchair, handed me a kidney basin, and off I went for x-rays. It was not his fault, since he was only carrying out his duty as an orderly.

It was early afternoon as I was wheeled from the ward and through the clinic. A throng of people were restlessly sitting and waiting to be seen by a doctor. The x-ray department was a fair distance from the main ward. To reach the x-ray department in the new addition, we had to pass through the crowded clinic.

The clinic resembled a train station. Many people were sitting in rows on the hard wooden benches, and some were at the canteen on the side of the lobby. Patients without the advantage of daycare brought their young children to their appointments, and often these children would noisily run around or cry. The very high ceilings and stone base floor amplified all these sounds. The clinic was a department where all eyes followed someone passing through.

All were anxiously waiting for their turn to see a doctor and fearful lest someone else get ahead of the queue. Seeing a doctor at the clinic usually meant spending several hours waiting and sitting on the hard and uncomfortable wooden benches. These people were anxious to see a doctor, pick up their prescribed medication from the hospital pharmacy, and leave as soon as possible.

During the week every department was constantly busy. The different clinics were dispersed throughout the hospital. People sat on chairs or benches along the walls of the hospital corridors until they were processed. The orderly left me with other people in the corridor of the x-ray department to wait for an x-ray attendant to call for me.

Soon I was brought into a room and asked to exchange my pajamas for the required x-ray gown. I tried to undress but I could not lift my arms. I did not have enough strength even to sit. Attempting to undress myself alone proved to be too strenuous. Overpowered by the large amount of medication, I lost consciousness. Sometime later I regained consciousness and found myself alone and on the floor. I felt awful. Trying to pull myself up on a doorknob, I fainted again. Eventually a technician came in and called for an attendant to help. The two helped me onto the x-ray table without changing my clothes or telling me why I was being x-rayed. Whatever x-rays were needed were taken, and finally another orderly wheeled me back to the ward and to my bed. A short while later I was given more pills, including Gravol. Now the pattern was set for the following weeks in this ward.

One afternoon the psychiatrist from the AMI strolled into the ward to see me. Although he was trying to conceal his Hungarian temper, he was extremely angry and wanted me to know how he felt. Having read through some of my medical history from my previous stay in this ward, he felt that I had omitted facts that I should have divulged to him in the therapy sessions.

What should I have told him that I had not already divulged? What secrets did I have? During therapy we discussed my problems and dreams and so many things that had happened to me while I was growing up. I certainly did not have an exclusive claim on problems. I only wanted what every other normal teenager in the fifties wanted. What more did he expect? I would find out soon enough what more information he had learned.

The NATO military doctor was no longer living in Canada. His research at the RVH was completed now that he had enough data for his report, and he had returned home. Copies of research he had acquired with patients of the ward were now on file for the benefit of the medical staff. These were the files the psychiatrist had read and was now referring to during his terrible outburst. Whatever had transpired during the truth serum sessions were never discussed with me, so therefore there was absolutely no way that I could tell anyone what so called secrets I had divulged under the influence of sodium amytal.

Weakness, depression, and my usual complaints were still with me. There was no end to this cycle. I felt terrible and looked horrible. I kept my arms covered to hide the ugly needle scars. My arms were tattooed by numerous blood tests. I looked like a junkie. And I still had hepatitis!

One morning during this bout of hospitalization, I was wheeled to another medical seminar. This was held in a very large room in one of new wings of the RVH. The large room and the fluorescent lighting made this room cold, intimidating, and unfriendly. Doctors and interns sitting around the large board table were already engaged in discussion of my case history. The results of numerous tests and analyses were reviewed while I sat uncomfortably at the end of the table. After a lot of discussion, a decision was reached and the conclusion drawn was that I was suffering from chronic and persisting hepatitis. It was decided that my next procedure would be a gastroscopy. As I was being wheeled back to my ward I could hear them charting more tests and a different variety of medications.

Several mornings later, I was wheeled out of the ward and taken to an operating theatre where the gastroscopy was performed. I was put to sleep with a general anesthetic. A large tube was then inserted down my throat and into my stomach. Hours later I awoke in the recovery room still drugged and very groggy. My whole body ached. My underwear was missing! What had they done to me? I was distraught and felt violated. I was modest, and objected to having my body seen or exposed, especially when I was not awake.

For the next couple of days nurses and doctors grinned whenever they saw me. It was a big joke. They knew something they were not telling me. Why had they removed my underwear? What they were not divulging was that they had also performed a prostoscopy while I was still under the influence of the anesthetic. I had not been told or prepared for the second test. For the next few days my whole body was stiff and aching from these two procedures.

My body was still examined at a whim or when a new medical student came into the ward. Many medical practitioners had seen and examined me but often I felt it was all so unnecessary. My body was still being probed, pushed, and tapped, and my skin pinched and checked for dryness and jaundice. I was sixteen and protective of whatever self-respect I had left. The fact that I had been misled about the procedures in the operating room made me extremely angry. I had been violated and left naked emotionally. This was a huge injustice to my personal dignity.

CHAPTER 8

HOME AGAIN, HOME AGAIN

Home again, home again! Back at the Allan Memorial everything seemed not to have changed in the least. I was back on the treadmill. Some staff changes were made but this was not unusual. Every three months we were subjected to a fresh batch of energetic medical personnel. They were the young student nurses and interns entering the dark corridors of the crazy house for the first time. Some patient changes were also apparent.

A mental institution must be like a dramatic stage play because each character/patient performs a different role. Day in and day out some cry and moan, while others display strange quirks like pacing in a dance-like pattern within the same area. Some do not speak at all, but stand against the wall like stage props the whole day, just starring blankly at their feet. If a patient leaves he or she is immediately replaced by another character, creating a new pattern to the scene. Of course ever-present cigarette smoke permeates the room, since smoking is the only activity in which these patients actively participate.

Two new characters entered the stage in this drama. A round and jovial little middle-aged fellow did not quite fit into this scene. He played two roles, one of a day patient at the hospital, the other as an M.C. in a leading nightclub, or so he would tell us. He kept company with most of the patients and especially enjoyed being in the company of young women. His energy was boundless. He was always telling jokes. Was he being treated? He did not seem to be on any medication or receiving ECTs. This was very unusual, especially as Dr. Cameron saw him regularly. Apparently the story was that the great responsibility and stress of a large family of six young children was the cause of this man's nervous breakdown.

Public transportation in the 1950's was the preferred travel mode in Montreal. Every day many patients including this squat little man would find themselves on the same bus. He would embark and later disembark in an old immigrant section of the city. This area was conducive to larger families because the old houses were much bigger than in most other areas. This could also have been low rental, but I somewhat doubted that this man had a financial problem, since he was always clean, well dressed, and carried large sums of money that he spent freely. This was also the era prior to the credit card so most people took money with them whenever they were out.

He would not hesitate to take a taxi if the weather was cold or wet. Treating people to coffee, cake, or anything else in the little coffee shop also gave him great pleasure. He enjoyed food and company and unlike everyone else, he was not lethargic or despondent. He even walked with a bounce. Sometimes he would disappear for hours and the staff never questioned his whereabouts. He had freedom without question, so what was his function at this institution?

The other character was an attractive divorcee with a small son. She was a nightclub singer who worked evenings at the same club as the man who had experienced a nervous breakdown. By the time she strolled into the hospital daily, the morning coffee and donuts were eaten or cleared away. So the coffee shop was her first stop. After signing in and taking her medication, she took up shop in the bathroom. Opening her case and displaying make-up, she proceeded to put the meticulously delicate and artistic application on her face. This was probably the most important part of her day. This was a long ritual and it took most of the morning to apply the make-up to her face. It was fascinating watching her do this application. Her clothing was always very attractive. A decorative matching hat hid a head of those metal curlers that were still used by women in the 1950's and 1960's.

McGill University In the 1950's was at the leading edge of education. Students from abroad were lured to acquire advance education at this prestigious Canadian institution. At that time McGill was known as the Oxford of Canada.

While on sabbatical, a young man and his wife from Ghana enrolled at McGill University. Arriving in time for the fall semester, these two young and eager students for the first time experienced the cold and gray depressing weather of a Montreal autumn. The weather, racial discrimination, isolation from family and friends, and the transition from Ghana to Canada became too extreme. The culture shock was insurmountable. The young woman succumbed to depression and was referred to the AMI. She was to become another victim of electro shock therapy.

One evening on arriving home from the day ward, I was transfixed by the television news being broadcast by a familiar voice. There was the godly head of the hospital, boasting about a new drug. He explained to the interviewer that depressed patients arrived at the hospital each morning. They were then given one of these wonder pills. In an instant these morose people miraculously had happy faces for the rest of the day. Side effects were not mentioned because the importance was the instant effect. This wonder drug referred to was Trofinal.

7   Experiments then may be performed on one man but within what limits? It is our duty and our right to perform an experiment on man whenever it can save his life or gain him some personal benefit. The principle of medical and surgical morality, therefore, consists in never on man an experiment which might be harmful to him in any

extent, even though the results might be highly advantageous to science, i.e. to the health of others...Claude Bernard, 1865.

Under no circumstances is a doctor permitted to do anything that would weaken the physical or mental health resistance of a human being except from strictly professional reasons in the interest of his patient.... A doctor is advised to use good caution in publishing discoveries. The same applies to the methods of treatment whose value is not recognized by the profession. World Medical Association Declaration of Geneva, 1948, under duties of doctors in general. (C. p. 211)

This was the 1950's. Patients were expendable. If a doctor felt like trying a new drug or method of treatment it was tried. Unlimited funds and patients were available to the AMI. Once a person was admitted and the forms were signed, then he or she was at the mercy of the physician to whom he or she was assigned.

Somewhere on the admitting form it was stipulated that a physician could try any medical procedure required to help the patient towards recovery. It did not matter what drugs or treatments were tried. If questioned, the physician would simply answer that he was doing everything possible for the recovery and well being of the patient. Patients were not allowed to complain or object. This was to help them get well. Did we not want to get better? It did not matter how painful the treatment or how horrible the side effects, the patient did not have the right of choice.

8   A mentally healthy society in Cameron's view would not have succumbed to the charisma of Hitler; it was psychiatry's mission to break out of the medical-disease model that had confined it to the treatment of the "sick" individuals and to reach the community-----<u>using research as its guide</u>----to ensure that society built personalities able to withstand the increasing stresses of modern life. (W. p. 110)

CHAPTER 9

WHAT IS REALLY GOING ON?

Who were these people that Dr. Cameron was trying to impress? They did not seem to be medical people, nor were they Canadians. Dr. Cameron was entertaining a delegation of very official looking Americans. Some patients and staff members felt an aura of suspicion and apprehension. We felt that whatever was transpiring with these official people would inevitably affect all of us either directly or indirectly. During the duration that these people were guests, they created a mysterious atmosphere of secrecy that hung like a heavy cloud over each one of us.

9   The TIMES magazine wrote describing a secret twenty-five year and twenty-five million dollar project---MKULTRA---designed to influence memory, thought, attitude, motivation, and ultimately human behavior. Several prominent psychiatrists were associated with these projects---one was Ewan Cameron. (C. p. 128)

#10   The CIA had a ready ally in Ewan Cameron. With the aid of an American working in Canada, caught up in the Cold War concerns, wanting to change society and with tremendous power and access to almost unlimited supply of subjects, the CIA funded brainwashing experiments from 1957 to 1960. (C. p. 140)

Many unusual people were visiting the hospital and observing the patients. These were the Americans. They were very well dressed in official looking dark business suits such as politicians might wear. They did not look, nor did they behave, like medical personnel. These Americans were frequently meeting in the stables with Dr. Cameron and a medical technician who was filming secret experiments on unsuspecting patients. The Allan Memorial was on exhibition.

The stables in another building were used as part of the hospital. The patients were told not to wander about while these people were visiting. We could not understand why someone was filming patients. The doctors were having frequent meetings. Something was definitely amiss. The staff was behaving differently and they were unusually reserved and quiet. They seemed to be checking and double-checking everything that they did. The atmosphere was so thick that it was like a dense fog hanging over the entire hospital.

This entourage divided their time between McGill University and the AMI. They spent considerable time with Dr. Cameron at the stables, in his downstairs offices, and in the privacy of the attic. The Dictaphone apparatus system was another source of interest to these guests. These machines produced tape recordings of psychotherapy-patient sessions that doctors had recorded. The receptionist regularly collected these tapes and typed them out specifically for Dr. Cameron.

Whatever was secretly being filmed was of great interest to these Americans. We wondered why these non-medical personnel were so interested in this specific medical facility and spent a good potion of time in the stable. They hardly spoke and when they did it was in hushed voices. Patients all had reasons for suspicion. We could not understand what was really happening, but we did feel that whatever it was would have a detrimental impact on us one way or another. What later would be revealed would be the funding agreement between the Canadian and American governments to do research with mental patients at the Allan Memorial Institute. These strangers worked for the American CIA, which was providing the funds for the promotion of specific research.

#11   The CIA funded Cameron's research from January 1957 to September 1960. (W. p. 138)

#12   FUNDING "due to the relatively limited resources of Canada, considerable thought has to be given to preventing duplication of effort with democratic countries. Any Canadian research program must therefore be integrated very closely with that of the United States, and it is Canadian policy to make facilities available to the United States if called upon, in furtherance of the common aim." (W. p. 46)

#13 ---The Provincial Deputy Minister of Health channeled all requests for funding and all disbursements for English-speaking researchers in the province through Dr. Cameron. (W. p. 117)

#14 The Allan was already getting enough money from American Defense sources: the U.S. Army, for instance, the sponsoring work on stress and on the drug Sodium Amytal at the Allan. The only Government funding in Canada that didn't fall to Cameron's charm was the Defense Research Board. (W. p. 118)

This entourage of visitors stayed long enough to disrupt the regular routine at the AMI. Many patients were directly involved, for they were being summoned to the stables for unknown reasons. The mental state of these patients was already unstable. All the drugs and treatments kept many patients disoriented. Some were suffering from schizophrenia and others were very depressed. In general, change and disruption of routine was traumatic to anyone who was at the AMI. Patients going to the stable went unwillingly and with trepidation. They did not enjoy their experiences and were always angry and agitated after each ordeal.

Although many of the patients at the AMI were not directly involved with Dr. Cameron, we wondered how we were all affected by the American funding to this institution. As the head of this institution, he was directly responsible for all treatments and medication for every patient.

Side effects to new drugs that were being administered were not a matter of concern. More intensive and more frequent ECTs were processed on an ever-increasing number of patients. Patients often appeared comatose and dysfunctional. Patient protests to treatments or any other complaints fell on deaf ears. We were told that doctors were here to help us get better and whatever method of treatment was tried was in our best interest. But was it really in the best interest of the patient, in the furtherance of medical science, or rather for more funds?

Monies dispersed to the Allan Memorial Hospital were to fund various experiments. There was no one Dr. Cameron had to report to or be accountable for in order to receive this funding. He invented the experiments and had others do the work. Every now and then the Americans would come to observe his masterpieces.

CHAPTER 10

THE SPRING OF 1959: HOPE

It was spring of 1959 and time for renewal. The trees were budding and beautifully exhibiting their majestic blossoms, while birds built their nests in preparation to lay their eggs. The flowers were pushing through the soft earth, finally making their debut after a long dormant winter rest. Sweet scents and fragrances of the different blossoms and flowers were wafting through and gently perfuming the air. It was spring, and somewhere in the future, just like my good health, was a new beginning for life and hope.

One day I discovered that I had enlarged glands at the nape of my neck. I was also covered in an itching red rash that resembled the measles. This was not the measles because I had had them when I was seven. My psychiatrist told me that it was probably a reaction to some medication and gave me some pills to relieve the itch. He finally stopped the nitrous oxide gas treatments but not the rest of the medication. Our psychotherapy sessions were still three times a week. Not very much had changed for me physically or emotionally.

#15 <u>Drugs</u>---chloropromazine---itchy and restless, both side effects of the drug. (W.p.155)

I was almost seventeen and my life was stagnant. Due to my illness I had missed a lot of school, whereas my friends had continued with their education and lives. Friendless and lonely, I was desperate for companionship. I wondered if this would be the pattern of my life. I was craving an education and wanted to go back to school. But how? Without the power of concentration, it would be almost impossible to study and learn. This was not the wonderful beginning for any young person who wanted to look forward to a full life. If I made it out of the hospital, where would I fit in society? I wanted to leave this institution and to try to lead a normal life.

It was the end of spring and everyone was preparing for final school exams. It was not an ideal time to go back to school. Rather than wasting a summer, I entered the work force. Finally arrangements were made through the hospital for me to work. I had a job with an insurance company during the summer months, beginning in May. But I had to promise to continue with my psychotherapy at the hospital, and continue to take all medications the doctor had prescribed.

The business section of the city was teaming with life. The area known as "Old Montreal" was the hub of all the large and major financial establishments, including bookstores, clothing boutiques, shoe salons, and many coffee shops. The huge old stone buildings, the hustle and bustling of people scurrying about, and the traffic noises were wonderful and exciting. They contrasted with the lethargic movements and silence of the depressing hospital atmosphere to which I had become accustomed. These people were alive, moving about quickly and energetically. A few people walked two or three together, chatting happily, adding to the hum and noises of the slow moving traffic. The street blocks were short and the stops at the intersections contributed to the slow moving traffic. This was quite a change from the familiar drugged environment to which I had become a part.

During these months I saw the psychiatrist regularly, except when he went away on vacation. That summer, Fidel Castro's brother invited the doctor and his family to visit with him in Cuba. Upon his return the doctor was in very high spirits and full of inspiration. Apparently Mr. Castro and Cuba were the impetus he needed to resume doing more intensive laboratory research at the AMI, and to continue practicing psychiatry.

I was working at an insurance company, earning money and making new friends, while still seeing the psychiatrist regularly after working hours. It was a quiet and peaceful walk from the office building to the hospital. After five o'clock in the afternoon, the hoards of working people all left at the same time, leaving this area of the city quiet and deserted. It would take me 40 minutes to slowly climb the hill up to the hospital for my required appointments. I continued to take the medication that was prescribed, because I did not want to jeopardize my opportunity to stay out of the hospital. Although the psychiatrist seemed pleased with my progress, he soon adjusted and increased my medication for no apparent reason.

My mind was not as alert as it should have been. I was becoming sluggish and was not functioning to my full mental capacity. The change in medication finally dealt its toll. One morning at work, I slipped and fell down the stairs. Thus ended my short working career. It had lasted two wonderful months and I should have been happy. At least I had had a glimpse of the outside world and the good life. This was a terrible disappointment for me. Was I cursed? Back I went to that splendid huge old Mansion on the hill, to the castle, to the gray walls, to my emotional cage at the Allan. Pills, pills, pills. So many. Every day.

Protesting to the psychiatrist was to no avail. As a matter of fact, he was upset that I would even entertain such a thought as to cut down on my medication. My vomiting had not been controlled and I was still very depressed. The medication was not always in my best interest as it caused horrible side effects, such as restlessness and severe shaking. Several times my skin erupted in an itchy rash, an obvious allergy to some of the pills. The doctor's answer was simple and to the point. I had the choice whether or not to take my pills. If I chose not to, the alternative was that I would to be sent to the Verdun Hospital. The Verdun Hospital was one of the provincial hospitals for the mentally ill. It had padded cells and all the windows had bars. Once admitted to Verdun, few people were ever discharged.

The doctors worked on a rotation system, spending three months in each department. Another three months had elapsed, and this meant that it was time for another change. Although my doctor was a gastroenterologist before escaping from Hungary in the early 1950's, he was now practicing psychiatry in Canada. He was very much involved with and working on different experiments in the lab. Now there would be a new doctor to whom I would be assigned at the AMI, a man who had recently arrived from Argentina.

CHAPTER 11

THE SLEEP ROOM

The summer weather in Montreal in August 1959 was unbearably hot and muggy. On the first Friday of the month I had booked my doctor appointment for the early afternoon, hoping to avoid the working crowd and heavy traffic of a hot day. It was the beginning of a very humid weekend, and on such days most people were anxious to get home quickly and away from the heat and smog of the downtown core. By booking an early afternoon appointment I could avoid the heat and crowds.

This Argentinian doctor spoke English with a slight Spanish accent. Short and slim, he looked more like a teenage boy than an adult. I knew nothing about him nor how he treated his patients. I approached this unfamiliar doctor's office with great fear and trepidation.

He introduced himself and told me that he had already made immediate arrangements for my admission as a full time patient at the AMI.

I would not be going home that afternoon! He explained that I had to be admitted into the ward as an in-patient, because on the following Monday I would begin sleep therapy. Someone from home could bring my toothbrush, toiletries, and whatever essentials I deemed necessary for the next couple of weeks. Then we spent the whole afternoon doing strange things in preparation for my admittance to sleep therapy.

His office was small and dark. Being on the east side of the corridor outside the ward meant that during the afternoon little sunshine, if any, penetrated his office. His overloaded desk faced the window and took up most of the width of the room. Equipped with a telephone, books, a chair, and a couch, the office had the necessities required of a psychiatrist. It was a great contrast to my last psychiatrist's spacious bright office on the sunny side of the building across the hallway.

On the same afternoon that I was admitted to the ward, another physician and researcher from Venezuela brought me to an unusual room. This darkened room contained a stool, a two-way mirror over a narrow shelf, and a little box close to the end on the right side of the shelf. The doctor placed a headband with a metal disc on my forehead. It was similar to the headband that an otolaryngologist or ear, nose, and throat doctor wears when examining a patient. He then placed me so I was facing the mirror. This was an observation mirror into the adjacent room. Then he left. I was not told why or what this was all about. Any questions remained unanswered. An hour or so later I was dismissed and sent back to the old ward on the second floor.

#16 A young Iranian doctor, Hassan Azima, had just come to the Allan from France where he trained under the French psychiatrist Henri Ey. Ey and others were experimenting with the new psycho-active drugs produced as a side-product of antihistamine research – chloropromazine was the first, - One of the things the French tried was to resurrect the old Swiss sleep therapy of the 1920's that had proved dangerous when achieved by barbiturates alone. Chlorpromazine combined with barbiturates, however, seemed to work; with careful nursing a patient could safely be kept in a chemical sleep for up to sixty-five days. Azima had brought the revamped sleep therapy with him to the Allan. (W. p.126)

South 1 was the ward that occupied the whole of the second floor in the old part of the original mansion. All the front windows faced Pine Avenue and overlooked the south part of the city. Walking into the ward, one noticed that the double doors opened onto a large hallway with the kitchen to the right, on the west side of the building. The sleep rooms and experiment rooms that were wired for sound were also along a short hallway, on the right wall of the kitchen.

The windowed nurse's station took up most of the front part of this section. The washrooms were on the left side after the entrance doors, before another hallway, and faced the nurse's station. The multi-purpose lounge/recreation/dining hall was on the south side of this hallway facing Peel Street, and a larger ward faced this room. This was the middle point of the building. I still did not know what was beyond this area. It led to another section of the old building providing more accommodation for patients.

Some patients, while they slept, were placed in a sleep therapy room off the main ward on the southwest side. The adjoining room to this ward was where I lazily slept away the month of August. My room was bright and sunny, but a heavy blind was always drawn to keep it dark. It had two beds, one on either side of the west-facing window. My bed was on the right. Each bed had a one-inch heavy board underneath the mattress. I thought this was unusual. My mattress, with that hard board beneath it, made my sleep extremely uncomfortable. Except for a few beds in the sleep rooms, all the other rooms had regular beds without boards.

Dinner in this ward was served at 5:00 p.m. both in the lounge and the main hallway. Four people sat at the card tables that were set up for each meal. At the end of the meal, a nurse handed everyone a cup of medication. Mine contained sixteen pills of different shapes in a rainbow of colours. While a nurse watched and waited, I swallowed these pills without being allowed any liquid.

Each day would become another hazy dream. I did not know when or how I got into bed that night.

After dinner I went to my room even though it was only 6:00 p.m. I drifted into the first abyss of sleep that would eventually last a month.

During visiting hours that evening I became aware of my mother's voice. She had brought my clothes and toiletries but was not allowed to see me. I would not be permitted to have visitors for the next few weeks.

The word in the day ward downstairs was out that I had been admitted to the sleep room. Flowers and chocolates in hand, one of the patients arrived early that evening to visit. Drifting in and out of a drugged sleep, I was aware of interrupted conversations. The chocolates and flowers were left with for the nurses to enjoy.

Suddenly it was Monday morning. Throughout the whole time that I was asleep, except for the first two days, I was always aware of the day, date, and approximate time of day. Three or four times a day I was given a colourful cocktail of pills in a small container. This was a combination of barbiturates, tranquilizers, and sleeping pills. A nurse always waited by my bedside while I swallowed them without any liquid. A kidney basin was also within reach. My need to vomit had not diminished, even during the sleep therapy.

Every day the standard procedure for each sleep patient was that an attendant wheel him or her to the washroom. Someone bathed us, brushed our teeth, combed our hair, and changed our clothes. Finally we were taken back to our beds. Like infants, we were totally dependent for our every physical need.

This whole time I was in an unconscious state, but if spoken to would reply. The Argentinian doctor brought in my meals daily and he personally fed me. He was doing research on Rapid Eye Movement (REM) while also analyzing my dreams. It was of great importance to him to know what they were all about. The incessant questions were always the same. What was the dream about? How long was the dream? The purpose of this therapy was to make me emotionally dependent upon the doctor. This is why he was the only person to feed me. In this way he endeavoured to eliminate all barriers so that my mind would be free, fresh, and clear. For the purposes of his studies he now had the opportunity to work on a clean slate.

#17   <u>PURPOSE –SLEEP ROOM</u> - people were drugged into sleep for days in there and given ECT until they didn't know who they were or where they were or how to feed themselves, until they lost control of their bladders and bowels. - Patients who had just come out of the sleep room standing in puddles of urine in the halls. Banging into walls as they tried to walk. (W. p.20)

My memory was very sharp. I felt that I could recollect details as far back as my birth. I could describe in detail incidents that happened within my first year of life. Was the purpose of this therapy to make me remember? Were these more experimental memory drugs being administered to me, or was this a continuation of a project on brain washing?

Experiments were being conducted on this ward, and some rooms were wired for video and audio. These wires were visible. There was never any effort to try to conceal them. Most patients knew about the experiments and were familiar with the pleasant nurse who was assigned to that area. She had been assigned to collect the data and worked for one of the doctors doing research. Her office was not on the ward but in the hallway within the same area as the laboratories. Specific research was being conducted in a specially reserved section of this ward. Here a male patient who was afflicted with Parkinsons, and a female patient sent temporarily from the Verdun Mental Institute, both had their rooms.

One night I was awakened from a deep sleep by an old man who was trying to climb into my bed. This was not a dream. This was very real. His gray hair was disheveled. His eyes were wild and his short Johnny coat, or hospital gown, was opened in the back and hanging off his shoulders. The disoriented man had lost his way trying to find the bathroom. My screams must have frightened him. A nurse who finally came to my rescue took care of him, and returned him to his bed in the other ward. I finally went back to sleep. It was during this period in the sleep therapy that I began hallucinating and having horrifying dreams.

I soon became aware that the bed next to mine was being borrowed for electroshock therapy. Every day medical staff accompanied Dr. Cameron as one by one he brought a number of patients into my room. The ECT machine was wheeled into the room after the patient was injected with an anesthetic. Probes were placed on the sleeping patient's temples and the current was switched on. The body on the bed would vibrate and jump. Now I understood why the heavy board was underneath the mattress. Once the procedure was completed, the sleeping patient was wheeled out. Another was immediately brought in. I would think to myself that they were having their brains "fried" in the process.

After my second week in the sleep room, I surmised that either my medication had been decreased or I had developed a tolerance to the drugs. I still slept, but my unconscious state now became semi-conscious. Patients scheduled for shock therapy were brought into my room for treatments. Still very drugged and dressed only in a thin hospital gown, I would be taken out of my room so I could not witness these procedures. I sat uncomfortably on a wooden chair either against the wall in the hallway, or in another sleep room. Here I could observe other sleep therapy patients who were in various stages of their treatments.

#18 The Allan, Cameron determined, was going to be an expression of the new way, from innovations in-patient care to the broadest possible spectrum of research labs.

(W. p.115)

In this sleep room most of the heavily drugged patients were wired to undergo "psychic driving" while they slept. There were different combinations and permutations of therapies rendered to patients. Some patients might have been in a supine position on a bed that moved up and down in a continuous motion. Others may have worn earphones through which recorded messages were continuously repeated. Some patients might have been blindfolded and had each of their limbs placed in a long cylinder tube, making it impossible for any body contact. This was called body deprivation therapy. Were these sleeping patients aware of what was happening to them?

#19 <u>BRAINWASHING PART OF THE EXPERIMENT</u>   The researchers prepared passages of propaganda in favour of innocuous theories they thought university-educated science students would be fairly resistant to; a belief in ghosts and extra sensory perception; and the anti-evolutionary point of view. "It is one thing to hear that the Chinese are brain-washing their prisoners on the other side of the world; it is another to find, in your own laboratory, that merely taking away the usual familiar sights, sounds, and body contacts from a healthy university student for a few days can shake him, right down to the base. (W. p.51)

#20 <u>THE SLEEP CURE</u>---putting patients to sleep using barbiturates for a period of weeks, a technique Cameron has been taught in Europe---was complicated by risk of bladder and lung infections. Cameron lists other things tried---carbon dioxide and oxygen treatment, acidosis, hyperventilation, ketogenic diet, his own heat and dehydration efforts. (W.p.88)

#21 Richard Helms in a 1953 memo he noted that part of its function was "implanting suggestions and other forms of mental control". MKULTRA was to move the laboratory testing on animals to testing on human volunteers (although the individuals were not necessarily to know what substance they were ingesting) and the use of experimental drugs on totally unknowing citizens. (C. p.127)

Three days had passed since I remembered emptying my bladder. The medication used during sleep-therapy must have slowed down my metabolism, or even stopped some of my natural body functions. I was given an injection and told that someone would come for me when I was ready to void. The shot should have taken twenty minutes to produce results, but within minutes my pillow was drenched in saliva. I could not control the dribbling from my mouth, a sudden condition that I was plagued with which would linger for many years.

I did not have a call bell at my bed. The only way to get the attention of a nurse was to shout for help. I tried to attract attention, but my voice was too weak. No one heard my pleas for help. The reaction to the injection took effect almost immediately. I had to hurry before I lost control of my bladder, so I attempted to make it to the bathroom on my own. The enormous consumption of drugs, lack of proper nutrition, and continuous sleeping had lowered my blood count and pressure considerably. As I tried to walk into the hallway, I fainted. The exertion was too great. Someone picked me up, sat me in a wheelchair, and helped me to the bathroom. For the next few days I was kept on intravenous feedings to prevent dehydration.

Visualizing and reflecting on this memory, I see a pathetic child huddled in sleep on the far side of the bed against a wall, wasting away the valuable and precious days of the short summer season.

CHAPTER 12

SLEEP THERAPY

The heavy humidity of that August and my inactivity contributed to a great deal of discomfort and pain. Whenever it was humid I would experience terrible bone pain. Even though I was in a drugged slumber, the pain would wake me so that extra blankets had to be put onto my bed.

At some point during a previous therapy session, I had revealed to the doctor that after my father's death I had been placed in an orphanage. I was only eleven years old. My mother decided to give away all my personal possessions. This included a favourite doll I had had since my early childhood. At the time I was very upset. This doll had a nostalgic importance to me as an emotional security blanket, and helped me hold on to childhood memories. That fragment of my past was horridly ripped from my life.

The Argentinean doctor had brought me a doll. It was a wonderful gesture on his part, but it was not the doll that I needed. I felt very alone having lost my father, and then being placed in a cold and unfamiliar environment away from family and friends. My situation was devastating. Losing that doll was like losing another part of myself, a part of my past that could not be replaced.

The table that was in the corner of the room was equipped with finger paints and paper. I was beginning to have extended periods of awareness and my waking days were getting longer. The doctor suggested that I should try finger painting when I felt alert. I did not enjoy the feeling of having wet and slimy cold fingers, but I did give it a try. The brown and yellow hued paints may have been the only colours available on the table, and they certainly are not my favourite colours today.

One day I saw another patient swinging the doll that the doctor had brought for me. Confused and unaware of her surroundings, this girl often took items that were in her path of vision. Confined to her room by a gate, she often managed to find a way out. The other patients always made a point of avoiding her. We were all aware that she was not responsible for her actions.

This young woman was part of a research project being conducted at the AMI. She was here on loan from the Verdun Hospital for experiments. Prior to an accident eighteen years earlier, she had been normal in mind and body. Now dysfunctional and mentally deficient, she wandered about disoriented, erratically tearing at her clothes and pulling at her hair. Her hands were in continuous motion and her behavior was bizarre. She existed in her own world, unaware and unaffected by people and her surroundings.

Her room was next to the sleep area in the main ward. The locked gate placed in front of the bedroom door should have kept her confined to her room. But she often managed to get past this barrier and every time she did, she was a source of tension and apprehension to the patients in our ward. Although we kept our distance, we never knew what was happening in her mind. She was just one more factor to deal with.

During my third week into sleep therapy, a new roommate arrived. She patronized her friend and neighbour Dr. Cameron, both of whose main residences were in Lake Placid, N.Y. On Dr. Cameron's suggestion that electro-shock therapy did wonders for people, she drove from the U.S.A. to the Allan every summer for her six to nine series of ECT treatments. They were very expensive, so she would remark, and she may have concluded that they must really do wonders. She did this voluntarily. What a choice! To spend one's vacation going from a luxurious U.S. border resort town to a mental institution in Canada did not make sense to me.

This buxom woman's loud snoring and uneven breathing frequently awakened me. She was a stout woman in her sixties. I knew that older people could die in their sleep of a heart attack. At my age, sixty seemed very old. It was frightening because at times she was not breathing and would enter what is now known as a stage of apnea. Quite often I would listen and wait for her to breathe again before allowing myself to go back to sleep. Her stay was short, only long enough for the required treatments. Then she was off again until the next summer. This was a great privilege for her and made her feel extremely honoured to be tended to by the famous Dr. Cameron.

Each morning the nurses, dressed in starched uniforms and caps, floated from ward to ward accosting every patient as they made their rounds. I always visualized these Florence Nightingales as swans because of their white starched uniforms and caps. Each nurse wore a pin emblem of the school from which she had graduated.

Did these women think that we were slightly deaf? Speaking loudly and slowly, the nurses subjected patients every day to the same canned verbiage and dialogue. "Do you know your name?" "What day is it?" "What month is it?" "How long have you been here?" I felt intimidated and infantilized each time that I was interrogated. These questions were repeated to almost everyone. This was a part of their job. But were nurses also fed a recording that was activated only when in the presence of a patient?

The evening nurses were much more relaxed. I guess the patients were not as frightening or intimidating. We were all fed sleeping pills as well as other medication, thus making us groggy and very docile. The doors to the ward were locked at night, preventing the heavily drugged and disoriented patients from wandering away.

The evening stresses were somewhat different for the staff because treatments were not conducted, technicians were not taking blood samples, and people were limited to their wanderings. It was a much calmer atmosphere. The lights were dimmed or altogether out. Everyone was subdued or sleeping, and patients did go to bed early. There was nothing else for the patients to do. Lights were out at 9:00 p.m. as a quiet stillness swept over the ward. If there were emergencies, patients were not aware, simply because we were too drugged to know or even care.

I had lost so much weight that I had become a live walking skeleton, all skin and bones.

Two of the new evening nurses were trying to "fatten me up". They would prepare for me the thickest possible calorie-laden milkshakes. Then they would proudly sit and watch me down their secret concoction, only to immediately try to provide me with another. The problem was that I could not keep much down. Whatever I did manage to absorb resulted in sever stomach cramps that were unbearably painful. The sheer volume of the icy milkshakes probably caused the cramps. Since my stomach had absorbed very little during the past few weeks, the milkshakes were more than my already sensitive and empty stomach could endure. These nurses were wonderful in thought and deed, but their method was lethal.

By the fourth week I was bathing and dressing myself. This was not an easy task. The simple exercise of stepping into a bathtub, trying to soap myself, climbing out, drying myself, and then trying to get dressed, was extremely exhausting. These seem like simple tasks, but at those moments the time and energy expended was unbelievable. It was an exhausting ordeal, and I always needed a few hours of rest to recuperate.

I did begin to notice that my daily energy level progressively improved. Eventually I felt that I was getting back to a normal level of strength, even though I still spent most of the day lying in bed.

People wandered about everywhere and did whatever they pleased. The in-patients were just as privileged as the day-patients. Only a few had restrictions. Of course, one could only function according to the level of medication. The staff was aware of this fact so were not concerned about how far, or where, a patient would wander. The occupational and art therapies in the main building, and other work activities such as cooking and pottery that were set up in the stables, were encouraged. Patients were everywhere, but only to the limitations of monitored sedation periods. By the end of the fourth week, the medication was beginning to wear off and I entered a transition phase of treatment.

September quietly and smoothly rolled in. Outside the yellow, green, and crimson leaves were gently falling. The cool breeze blowing from the side of the mountain carried a wonderful scent of the pine and fir trees.

The Allan was built on the south side of Mount Royal. It overlooked the city of Montreal that was spread out below the grounds to the southwest of the Royal Victoria Hospital and the St. Lawrence Harbour. This was indeed a Royal sight.

Many sleep therapy patients who had been admitted at about the same time as I was had already been discharged. The bed beside me was not occupied, except by patients undergoing their daily routine shock treatments after breakfast. I was not permitted to stay in my room to witness anyone undergoing ECTs. This gave me the opportunity to circulate among the other patients from across the sleep room and beyond the east hallway. But because I was still very weak, I spent most of my waking day sitting on top of my bed dressed in "regular" clothes.

Daytime in the ward was filled with the hustle and bustle of the nurses and technicians trying to locate certain patients, giving them medications, taking them for ECT treatments, or taking their regular blood tests. Nurses knew who went to the various occupational departments, but occasionally there was pandemonium when a patient went missing.

Patients were famous for taking off, especially if they were scheduled for unwanted treatments.

The mornings were short. At 11:30 a.m. the main hallway and the recreation rooms were set up with tables and chairs for lunch. The mixing of the food with the basic sterile hospital odours created a strange combination of smells. Lunch at noon was always a large meal. We sat where we pleased and with whomever we chose. For the next forty-five minutes we ate while nurses dispensed medication. People either talked or sat in silence, cried, laughed, or both. This was the good part of the day.

After lunch the day took on a different atmosphere. The patients were a little more subdued than before having had lunch. Group therapy, board games, cards, or bed rest was encouraged. Some patients continued with the occupational therapy activities they had already been doing, while a few would frequent the downtown area of St. Catherine Street. They might shop or browse, or meet with an old friend and have coffee at the old Murray's cafeteria across from St. James Cathedral. The remaining patients wandered aimlessly, not doing or thinking, just existing. We had a snack break at 2:30 p.m. and visitors from 3:00 p.m. until 4:00 p.m. Supper was at 5:00 p.m.

After supper, the accumulation of medication caused patients to be in an even quieter mood than in the afternoon. Many made themselves ready for bed. Some had lights out before 9:00 p.m. By that time we had all had a full day. The evening visiting hour was from 7:00 p.m. until 8:00 p.m. and most of us were so exhausted that we were happy to get ready for bed. Hospital life was not very exciting or stimulating. One day was the same as the next. Faces sometime changed, but not the routine.

Dreary, cold, and windy, October descended for us physically as well as emotionally. All the leaves had fallen and were spread on the ground like a thick coloured carpet. The naked trees stood solemnly like dead, rigid skeletons around the hospital. The sounds of the ships blowing their horns as they passed through the harbour throughout the night were haunting.

At night the wooden floors creaked in the old building. The soft howling sound of the wind through the ward, and the blowing horns of ships as they passed through the harbour, were both haunting and a little eerie. Most of us were oblivious to these sounds because of our heavy intake of drugs. If we had to go to the washroom during the night we would go with some apprehension, and only if we really had no choice. If the building really was haunted, our beds offered some emotional security against the unknown elements.

CHAPTER 13

ALL THE WORLD'S A STAGE

Instead of being discharged from the AMI, I was transferred to the main ward on the east side of the building. A variety of characters inhabited this ward, including one young woman who had been in and out of the hospital for many years. Comfortably sitting in a nook in the main hallway day in and day out, she would knit continuously, anything from a simple scarf to a complicated suit. Knitting was her passion and an easy escape into her thoughts. This allowed her the privacy of not having to interact with people while she was counting stitches. By sitting in the same corner everyday and working at her hobby over the past few months, she had completed a new winter wardrobe for herself.

Manic depression had qualified this passionate knitter to be a permanent resident at the Allan. For more than two years, she had been subjected to several insulin-shock therapy treatments that were processed over a period of several weekends.

Now she was periodically having a series of ECTs, as well as the drugs and psychoanalysis for which all Allan residents qualified.

A single young woman of nineteen felt that her refuge was the Allan. In the fifties most single young girls lived at home either with parents or with family members. This young girl was extremely angry that her parents had divorced and did not want to go home to either parent. Her parents would visit daily but separately. Every afternoon her mother would bring a home baked cake, and every evening her father would arrive with a smoked meat sandwich. She shared and enjoyed the goodies but complained about and objected to her parents. She preferred the company of the patients at the Allan. Her passion was to smoke a cigarette while chewing gum, and talk while she played monopoly or cards.

Another patient had a phobia about personal cleanliness and body odour. Most of the day she spent taking showers, and then going from person to person asking if she still had an odour. Her favourite past time was slashing her wrists. This was her third admittance to the sleep ward and she was hoping it would be the last. The duration of her therapy was always three weeks in sleep therapy and a series of nine ECTs. She did not seem as affected as most sleep patients because she was coherent and knew who she was and why she had been admitted. She left the hospital after her last set of ECTs and returned home to her parents.

An elderly man who was afflicted with Parkinson's disease was a permanent resident in this ward. His slow unstable walking and continuous shuffle qualified him for permanent hospital attention. This once vibrant and intelligent family man had once worked as a successful engineer. He played chess regularly but was very slow and limited his conversations to grunts. It was terribly pathetic to see this shell of a man, for though his mind was still active and aware, he was beyond having any semblance of conversation.

A woman in her late forties was probably going through her menopause. Dr. Cameron was her personal physician. She despised both the doctor and the private nurse he had assigned to her. The nurse was severe, mean, and terrifying. During the day this nurse sat playing cards, taking verbal abuse spewed at her by her charge. This middle aged patient found it to be poetic justice that while she had been raising her children, she often kept them amused by playing cards with them. Now she was being kept entertained by this despised nurse in much the same manner that she had kept her children amused. The daily routine of playing cards to keep the patient occupied always ended with this woman violently flipping the cards off the table. Shouting profanities in resistance, the lady would be forcibly dragged back to her room to be sedated by the nurse.

This private nurse only worked with Dr. Cameron's patients, but occasionally on his instructions this nurse also worked nights on the ward. It seemed that my nightmares and hallucinations were prevalent only when she was on duty, and I was frightened by her presence. She was most likely working if and when LSD was used on this ward as far as I could surmise.

My nightmares were always the same. I felt that I was continuously being flung into a massive sticky spider web over and over again. I tried to scream for help but could not make a sound. I always remember this nurse being present whenever I awoke after the nightmare.

#22   DREAM – zigging and zagging around like a squirrel in a cage. I couldn't get out. I tried to climb the walls. (C. p. 14)

A young depressed woman who had recently given birth was another patient in this ward. She resisted and refused treatment and tried to leave the hospital to go back home to her children and husband. But Dr. Cameron pleaded with her, telling her that he knew what was best for her. He always had his way and this young woman finally and resentfully allowed herself to be subjected to more treatments. This poor woman often fell asleep even while dressing. It was not unusual to find her on the floor naked and asleep. She was always being dragged away for treatments crying, begging, pleading, fighting, and kicking. It was always such a sad and pathetic scene. As often as possible she tried to run away through the woods behind the hospital, only to be brought back again for more intensive ECTs and drugs. The patients all knew what was happening, and we were apprehensive lest Dr. Cameron get his clutches on us as well. We all feared him but we really did not know why.

A young man of nineteen felt obliged to stand against the wall and hold it up. No one knew why he was here, and everyone was curious to know what problems had brought him to the Allan. He did not make any sounds. For hours he simply leaned against the wall in the corridor, staring at his feet. This was his activity until his family arrived at visiting time to gently urge him back to his room. This pathetic soul was beyond resisting treatments.

A fourteen-year-old grade nine student appeared coherent and friendly with the other patients. Her family physician referred her to Dr. Cameron because she felt very nervous whenever she had to write exams at school. She could not understand why Dr. Cameron had had her hospitalized. Her problem was not visible or obvious and she seemed normal. The only complaint was that she was a little nervous at times. Many people for various reasons are occasionally nervous, especially about writing exams. This girl seemed well until she started her ECTs. I never saw her again. The rumour was that one day when approached by Dr. Cameron, she started crying hysterically. She was so traumatized by seeing him, she accidentally bit off one of her little fingers.

Crutches, kidney basins, chairs, shoes, or anything else within grasp would be flung in any direction. Anger, frustration, and a sense of futility would cause a pretty eighteen-year-old patient to have frequent violent outbursts by throwing anything she could manage to pick up from the area around her bed. She was stricken with Multiple Sclerosis, a horrible disease for anyone to suffer. The disease was progressing rapidly, keeping her confined to a wheelchair. The bag and catheter connected to her were constant reminders of her fate. She felt imprisoned within her body. Her mind was alert and aware of everything that was happening to her. This was an unfair sentence, and it was not surprising that she was extremely angry and upset at what destiny had given her to bear.

The routine in the in-patient ward was similar to that of the day ward. Once or twice a week the blood technicians, vampires as far as I was concerned, would set up shop in a little room. After lining up the victims they collected the precious vials of blood. I guess the blood tests provided information as to whether or not we inmate-patients were faithfully swallowing all our medication.

Most of the patients had ambivalent emotions. We wanted to leave the hospital and get as far away from it as possible. We could not endure any more treatments. But we had all become so dependent on the security of the hospital environment that we were terrified of what awaited us on the outside. Where else would one be catered to so well?

The breakfast alone could feed someone for a whole day. How many people on the outside enjoyed coffee or tea, fresh heavy cream for hot or cold cereal, eggs, bacon, jam, and toast with marmalade, honey, and peanut butter? Every breakfast table was adorned with hot and cold milk, hot cocoa, coffee, tea, and juice for all to enjoy. The other meals were just as elaborate and plentiful. Snacks, sandwiches, beverages, and cookies were served every afternoon. Another snack was provided before bedtime. This was more like an expensive resort hotel rather than a mental institution. This seemed like a warm and comfortable setting from the outside, but what was really happening on the inside?

For a short while I shared a room with two girls. It was much more interesting than always being alone. Leisure time and mundane conversation with drugged and heavily sedated individuals helped to create a more tolerant means of floating through the day. There were no true friendships, for all we had in common was that we were not well people. Unfortunately this arrangement was not to last. A private room was available to which I was transferred. I had not asked to be moved and I did not like it. To her chagrin my new roommate had to adjust to two new patients.

CHAPTER 14

REALITY

#23   <u>ISOLATION</u>   The basic McGill perceptual – isolation experiment – alone on a comfortable bed or couch in a quiet room – eyes were covered with goggles that allowed diffused light but no pattern; arms were covered to the tips of the fingers with cardboard tubes, so that though they still had some mobility, they didn't have much sense of touch, The room was miked so that if they hummed, or talked or thrashed restlessly the researchers could hear them. They wore headphones that delivered either 'white noise" or inane ditties, like the sixteen bars of "Home on the Range" repeated several times, passages from a religious primer for six –year-olds, numbers, and nonsense syllables. (C. p. 50)

The Argentinean psychiatrist must have had a deadline to complete certain experiments. He used one of his young female patients as his subject, and placed her in the experimental and research area beside the sleep therapy ward.

The special nurse monitored this area audibly and visually. The room was especially prepared for this experiment. The windows had been blackened, heavy blinds were drawn, and the walls and the door were padded. All this was to eliminate light and noise from the outside. The only piece of furniture was the single bed in the middle of the room. This young girl was being treated to "Body Deprivation."

Blindfolded, with each limb in a large cylinder, the girl was left alone for two weeks in a dark, unfriendly, and soundproof cell. The doctor would take in her meals at sporadic intervals, thus trying to confuse the date and time of day for her. But somehow she did manage to attract the attention of some of the patients by banging on the bottom of the door. They provided her with cigarettes but I do not know if she managed to remove the cylinders so that she could smoke. Of course this was not allowed. It defeated the purpose of the experiment. She survived the ordeal, only to have it repeated again a few weeks later.

My new room was in the oldest section of the mansion, in the northeast side facing south towards the St. Lawrence River. This was around the corner from my previous ward but it was quite different. This room was once part of the billiard room that had been divided to add a few more bedrooms, while still keeping a much smaller billiard room for patient recreation. Billiards was something like the game of pool or snooker, and many of the patients were familiar with the game. The billiard room was the focus in this area and patients, friends, and their families spent many enjoyable hours playing around this table.

Electrical wires that led into my bedroom disappeared into the wall. It made me extremely uncomfortable knowing that my every move and sound was being recorded. All the rooms in this section were private and all the patients belonged to Dr. Cameron. What was I doing here? The stairwell across the hallway and behind the door led up to one of Dr. Cameron's private offices. He was the only person we saw coming and going from this part of the attic. It was closed off from staff members and technicians in other departments who used the attic from the other side. None dared to wander into Dr. Cameron's territory. It was off limits to all. This was his private and personal territory.

Another of Dr. Cameron's ongoing patients who experienced depression and insomnia was slated for ECT treatments. Every night before going to bed, she was given a foul smelling green fluid to drink that she claimed was the only medication that finally allowed her some sleep. Paraldehyde was that atrocious smelly green liquid. The fumes emanated from her and lingered through the hallways she passed as she went to her room. This foul smelling substance lingered on her breath and penetrated through her skin even into the following day. It was not pleasant to be in her presence.

The doctor wanted to be innovative with my treatments, so he decided he needed to try hypnosis. He would tell me to relax and lie down on the couch, and concentrate on a crystal disc he swung back and forth in front of me. I was supposed to feel tired and sleepy. Instead I became agitated after a session of this so-called hypnosis. I felt used and degraded. Any questions I asked of the doctor were never answered. Whether or not

I actually ever was hypnotized was never made clear to me despite his evasive explanations. I do not recall ever having had loss of time, and I felt that I was always aware of what I was saying and doing. When I asked if I had been hypnotized, because I felt that I had not, he would not answer. Instead he would tell me that one day I should write a book about these experiences. His three inch thick file on me was getting still larger.

Three months had already elapsed since my admission to the Allan for sleep therapy. November dragged in gray, cold, and humid. I was still a patient in South 2. I had become more and more dependent on the drugs and security of the hospital environment. It was safe and warm, and I was not lacking in physical needs. I had no responsibilities. If I did not keep my food down after taking medication, I was given more pills. If I was over medicated it was not a big deal because I could sleep it off. If this occasionally happened no one seemed to worry about it. These overdoses would lower my blood count and leave me very weak for a few days.

There were a few bright days in an otherwise cold, dull, gray November. Once a week I was given a pass with permission to go home for the day. These were good days and I enjoyed the outings. It was a change of environment and atmosphere. I saw people in a different way. They were alive, moving, and talking, doing things for which I did not have the energy. I did not know if I would ever cope again living on the outside with normal people. For now I had become accustomed to the safe haven that the hospital environment still provided.

The dependency and comfort that the hospital provided was also frightening. Is this where I would spend the rest of my life? I had to leave. Finally in early December I took the plunge. I had to go home eventually. Collecting my bag of pills with a promise to take them faithfully, and with a confirmed appointment to see the doctor in a few days, I was discharged. I needed to go back to the reality of the normal world to try and pick up where I had left off. I thought that I would try to live as normal a life as possible. It was difficult because my energy level remained at an extremely low ebb. Trying to cope with menial tasks and activities made me aware of how much I had once taken for granted. My patience suffered. I had little tolerance for everyone around me and I was very lonely.

After that horrible incident with her boyfriend, my mother decided not to marry. We moved from the apartment and into a house with other relatives. My sister was still in elementary school, and needed adult supervision while my mother was at work. This was the best arrangement that could be made at the time.

Being in hospital for such an extended period of time made fitting into a normal milieu quite upsetting. My sister was embarrassed by my skeletal appearance and did not want her friends to see me. Because we had not really grown up together we had little in common. She rejected me as an unwanted stranger invading her space. I no longer had school friends because they were still active and busy with their studies and expanding their personal interests.

The interim year and a half between leaving Summerhill House, the Home cum Orphanage, and trying to continue in a different high school until my illness when I was hospitalized, was long and lonely. I tried to resume a relationship with the friends from grade school prior to my father's death, with whom I had managed a superficial relationship while I was still attending school. Now these friends were no longer around. I had no peers or anyone to talk to, and without the ability to concentrate I could not read. I was a textbook case of depression.

CHAPTER 15

A NEVER ENDING CYCLE

The December air was cold and humid. The skies were often dark and overcast, and the packed snow made walking on the sidewalks difficult. I was not able to cope with the damp and chilly weather so I stayed indoors most of the time. After leaving the hospital I tried to adjust to living in a family setting with people who were not medicated or programmed. It was different and difficult. These people were alert and active, while my mind was sluggish and my movements lethargic. The few day passes of the previous month had not prepared me for this enormous let down.

The ceilings in the hospital were high and there was space to move about. At home the eight and a half foot ceiling and standard room size were confining. I had become accustomed to larger spaces so it required several days for me to adjust. I still continued to have uncontrollable bursts of depression.

It was a year since I had been first admitted to the Royal Victoria Hospital. I was declared free of hepatitis, so why was I still suffering? My medication was being taken appropriately and it was impossible for me to do little other than rest. I did not require food to be exciting or creative. The bland hospital diet that I had become accustomed to left little imagination to stimulate any palate. I was underweight and malnourished due to my lack of appetite, and kept down very little of whatever I did eat. The strange jaundice tint of my skin certainly did not make me attractive. In fact my sister complained about me and was embarrassed by my very existence. Not only was I suffering physical and emotional pain, but now I felt I was an added burden to the family.

My bursts of depression and my physical appearance greatly disturbed my grandparents as well. Convinced that a change of people and scenery may help, or at least could not do any harm, they decided to take me along with them to Toronto to attend a family wedding.

I had not ventured from Montreal before, because the cousins we would be staying with always came to visit us. Everyone was happy that we were finally taking a trip. It was wonderful. Choosing gifts, buying new clothes, and planning ahead were new and wonderful experiences for me. It certainly was exhilarating, a breath of fresh air into my monotonous existence. This would be a real adventure that I was looking forward to with great enthusiasm.

At that time, the trip from Montreal to Toronto was about a nine-hour train ride through the night. Many people still chose to ride rather than fly. Toronto was exhilarating. It had less snow and humidity than we had in Montreal, and the temperature was slightly warmer. For a few days before the wedding we met with our relatives, and traveled around the area sightseeing and meeting other cousins. Unfortunately I could not keep up with this pace. Instead of getting stronger I kept getting weaker, and I still experienced sudden bursts of depression. My concerned grandparents decided to shorten our visit. We returned to Montreal soon after the wedding, a week ahead of our arranged time.

A promising December lapsed into a dreary January. The unending gray rolling clouds and continuous snow were enough to keep anyone depressed.   January 1960 was another New Year with a different beginning, but still held no apparent change in my health. With all the medication and regular psychotherapy, I should have felt better and less depressed. But instead of getting well, I found myself admitted back at the RVH with hepatitis. Nothing had changed. I was in a whirlpool. It was a never-ending cycle.

CHAPTER 16

BIOPSY

Montreal was a metropolitan center and at that time the most populated city in Canada. Air transportation and ocean liners promoted easier and more pleasant travel from abroad, creating new post war immigration and tourism. Montreal was an exciting and world-class city. The influx of a variety of different nationalities, languages, customs, and new foods added to the colour and charm of the city. A large influx of foreign immigrants meant more and different diseases, and exotic and unfamiliar ailments being exhibited in Canada.

McGill University, affiliated with the Royal Victoria Hospital, was attracting many foreign students. Both these modern facilities were renowned, reputable, and favoured teaching institutions, drawing the most cleaver academic and medical students from different parts of the world. They eventually would take back this knowledge to their respective countries.

A great deal of construction and expansion was being done simultaneously at the RVH and at McGill University. Physical changes to the building were always in progress, creating a constant level of chaos. New wings and more wards had been added to the RVH. The old medical wing was converted into different departments. The medical ward was now in the new addition. Various research and test processing laboratories were added. More operating theatres were built where additional surgeries could be performed. This hospital was rapidly becoming the institution for advanced medicine, and fostered leading edge research scientists in Canada. There was always a batch of innovative new interns who nevertheless still maintained some of their old school medical education practices.

Within the first few days of my admittance to the RVH I was subjected to my first liver biopsy. Results of a blood test suggested to the doctor that the massive amounts of barbiturates and tranquilizers I was taking might have affected my liver. I was oblivious then as to the reason to have to go through such an experience. I still wonder years later why this procedure was necessary.

The thought of a biopsy of any nature is frightening and traumatic for a patient. It is a small surgical procedure but care against infection has to be maintained. Liver biopsies were not frequently performed. Therefore many doctors learning this medical procedure were excited and anxious to participate on a live person, having only seen it done on cadavers.

The liver biopsy was a terrible experience. A sterile solution was wiped over my exposed stomach. A local anesthetic was administered underneath the disinfected skin area. The doctor in charge explained this relatively simple technique to the entourage of anxious onlookers who had gathered around my bed. He did not perform the biopsy, but rather gave the honour to one of the excited young interns.

These anxious students were told that this was considered a simple and minor operation. However it could prove dangerous or life threatening due to hemorrhaging if the patient moved when the surgical probe was inserted. I was instructed to lay still and remain calm. I was assured the procedure would not hurt and would be over quickly.

With trembling hands and unsure movements, the anxious young intern seemed to lack confidence. I thought he looked a little frightened. He slowly inserted the long hollow needle between my ribs until it reached its goal. Then a small piece of liver the size of a pea was snipped off, pulled out, and placed into a container with sterile solution.

My body was taut throughout the whole procedure. I was nervous and frightened and tried not to move. The anesthetic did not freeze the liver. It was only the surface of the skin that was anesthetized. The intensity of the throbbing pain was similar to that of a rotting tooth being extracted. The extracted liver was quickly immersed into a vial containing a sterile solution and sent off to pathology to be analyzed. The interns hurried off to return to their daily rounds, relieved that the surgery was a success.

To prevent the possibility of hemorrhaging I had to remain still for the next twenty-four hours. Again I had been used, lied to, and abused. It did hurt!

Now I had to keep still and lay flat, with only a thin layer of gauze wrapped around my ribs as a grim reminder of my purpose. That day I was an object for the use of medical advancement. It was unfair and I certainly did not like being subjected to unnecessary pain.

This liver biopsy was a lesson for the young interns and medical students present. Was this procedure really necessary? Was this exercise for my well-being to discover why the hepatitis re-occurred, or was I being used as a learning tool for the furtherance of medical students and science?

Injections were still a common and every day occurrence. I felt as though any time anyone on the medical staff felt the urge to find a pincushion, they would be attracted to me. So it was not unusual for a nurse to come in to give me an injection even during visiting hours. I was given one particular injection, which I believe was a mixture of stelazine and chlorpromazine. This mixture of medication was not on my regular list of daily drugs.

Almost immediately the muscles all over my body, including my facial muscles, began twisting and contorting. My jaw felt dislocated. My now enlarged and thickened tongue hung out of my mouth and flopped from side to side. This caused severe pain. My eyes rolled back into my head, giving me an excruciating headache. My back arched. I felt a terrible pressure and surge of pain on my spine as it was jerked backward. My limbs felt like they were being pulled off in four different directions at the same time.

All my muscles ached from the strain. Calling for help was useless. The nurse who administered the shot insisted that nothing could be done to help. She did not know why this was happening and told me there was nothing to help ease the pain or relieve the contortions.

#24 Largactal (chlorpromazine) The downside – the drugs could cause permanent Parkinsonian-style brain damage. (W. p. 163)

The curtains around my bed were discretely drawn, so as not to upset or agitate the other patients and visitors present in the ward. During the next few hours I must have looked like a wooden marionette being manipulated by a drunken operator. I lay in my bed trying to be still, praying for relief. Several hours later the majority of the drugs had dissipated from my system. However the side effects left my muscles stiff and aching for many days afterwards.

Why did this have to happen to me? Was it due to the drugs, or had I contracted another disease? The medical staff behaved as though this was an unfortunate, isolated occurrence, and not really a problem. Eventually I did stop thinking about it.

#25   Effects of chloropromazine – Allergic reactions, jaundice and liver damage, nausea and "epigastric distress", a wooden "Parkinsonian" appearance, low blood pressure and irregular heart rhythms, dry mouths and noses, and a general interference with mucous production that rendered patients susceptible to colds, --- abnormal muscle reactions, -dystonias – or uncontrollable and painful cramps – from spasms in the eye muscles that lock them in a fixed upward stare, to wry neck, in which the neck muscle contract to pull the chin toward one shoulder or the other, to muscle seizures in the lower back; to life threatening spasms in the mouth and throat that interfere drastically with breathing. (C. p. 183)

In late 1950 Florence Nightingale was a waning memory.   Nevertheless one remnant of that era was still in practice. Every night before putting out the lights, nurses went from bed to bed with rubbing alcohol and talcum powder to give each patient a back rub. Patients were very appreciative. In general all the nurses were pleasant and caring with the patients in their charge. This nightly ritual, along with a sleeping pill, was soothing, comforting, and relaxing. It did help patients go to sleep. At that time, that exercise was as much a part of the nurse's daily routine as was taking blood pressure, pulse, heart rate, and temperature.

During my fourteen days in hospital there was little rest. Doctors, interns, and residents made daily rounds. Bed rest was always recommended. A variety of diets, drugs, and daily tests were part of a regular routine. Most patients suffered daily blood tests, urine analysis, x-rays, and routine examinations by doctors and interns. Biopsies were performed only on certain patients. These orders for biopsies were given only when a specific disease or condition was suspected, such as kidney stones or tumour, sclerosis of the liver, hepatitis, or other serious illness.

I had recuperated sufficiently after the liver biopsy and subsequent muscle contortions. Two weeks later I was discharged from the RVH to again return to the AMI. Like the majority of patients, I left the RVH after having had a battery of tests performed, a regime of medicine prescribed, and an appointment made to see a doctor within the next two weeks. The few who did remain were usually terminally ill and stayed until they died.

CHAPTER 17

ALWAYS IN CONTROL

Returning to the Allan should have meant a step towards my improvement. I had just recuperated from another attack of hepatitis. Psychotherapy and drugs were still the basic methods of treatment. My body was so saturated with chemicals that it did not feel connected to my mind. I saw, felt, and did. I was looking out from within and did not care about anything. I let things happen, and when I was told to do something, I reacted like an obedient child. It did not matter whether I wanted to do what I was told, but I followed instructions. The drugs had their effect on my will and I was totally dependent on the medication.

Everyone expected that I would die. My mother was told that I was dying of an unknown, incurable, and deteriorating disease. There seemed to be no hope for my recovery. Everything being done was for my benefit. The doctors were in the dark and did not really know what was causing the chronic and persisting hepatitis, or why my vomiting could not be controlled by medications that had already been tried.

As time went on I did become physically stronger. The art therapist finally encouraged me to do charcoal drawings and oil painting. But it was still difficult for me to concentrate for any prolonged period of time. The sound of the music in the art room was always so soothing, helping to ease the pain and void that I continuously felt.

My mind would still wander, and now I was beginning to think about my former school friends. What were they doing now? I wanted to go back to school, to be a regular teenager, and be normal. But it was not meant to be. Not just yet at any rate!

Patients were always coming and going. A new, young, pregnant, and very depressed woman arrived. Her husband was away in the American Army and they had spent very little time together since their marriage. Dr. Cameron was treating her with ECTs, psychic driving, and a new drug. She did not like it, but resolved herself to the fact that maybe it was good for her. Instead of getting better, she started to hallucinate, became more depressed, and soon started acting violently. She was confined to her room like a prisoner locked in a cell.

It seemed that Dr. Cameron's personal patients all suffered the same treatment: electro-shocks, psychotherapy, psychic driving, and hallucinatory drugs. All pleaded, complained, and begged against the treatments. Dr. Cameron was threatening but was always in control, and he knew how to coerce each of his patients. In the presence of the attendants, he would speak in a soft, convincing, and controlling tone. He explained that he only wanted what was in the best interest for each patient's recovery. The broken, distraught, and confused patients, out-numbered by Dr. Cameron and his attendants, never had a chance. Reluctant and crying, the patient finally conceded to defeat and went unwillingly for the dreaded treatment.

Many patients ran away when they knew that Dr. Cameron was coming, only to be forcibly brought back and confined. The sedation medication to the patient was heavier after such an episode. I was thankful that I did not have personal contact with this man, even though he was indirectly in control of my treatment. Whatever treatment any doctor at the Allan decided for each patient was assessed under the close scrutiny of Dr. Cameron.

#26   Given Cameron's published concerns, was this, ironically, just a recapitulation of what happened in Nazi Germany --- a man with great power is not stopped by his underlings? Or did his colleagues simply not know what was taking place? The experiment ended, but for the victims and those who love them, the pain continues. (W. p.141)

Largactil, Phenobarb, Phenobarbital, Trilafon, Equinil, Etrafon, Gravol, Nembutal, Trofanil, Stemitil, Triavil, Seconal, Stelazine, Sernyl and Nitrous Oxide gas were samples of the drugs that I was given. Sometimes I would have a cocktail of up to sixteen pills at a time, but that did not seem to alleviate the problem. It was not a surprise when I once again was admitted with hepatitis back to the RVH medical ward.

CHAPTER 18

STEMATIL

The ward in the new building was very different from the original ward. Most rooms had four beds, some had two, and a few were private. The walls were painted in soft colours and the lighting was subdued, in contrast to the bright lights and sterile atmosphere of the rooms in the original old building. These rooms were quite different. The old ward was probably fashioned after the original Florence Nightingale ward, whereas here each bed was equipped with a call bell and a small ear radio. It was a much warmer and friendlier atmosphere. Being able to listen to the radio helped to sooth away many, but unfortunately not all, discomforts.

Wanting to know about the drug Stematil was of special interest for one of the new interns. His main interest was with the after-effects of the drug, so my body was the chosen recipient of his experiment. His requirement was to know the duration, reaction, and side effects of the drug.

Whatever happened to the patient did not really matter. It was important to know what this drug would do.

The effect was almost instantaneous. The injection caused my tongue to become enlarged, my jaw to distort, my eyes to roll back into my head, and my muscles to go into complete contortions and spasmodically jerk. I felt like a pretzel. This had happened to me once before when I was previously in this ward. It was a very painful ordeal and again I begged for help.

This time the nurse told me that I could not have the antidote, because the doctor wanted to know how long it would take for the drug to wear off. Apparently this was the same culprit drug responsible for the contortions I had experienced the previous January. I could take Stelazine orally without noticing negative side effects. This allergic reaction only happened when I was injected with Stelazine or Stematil, or when they were mixed with another drug. This experiment was tried one more time with the same painful effects. I was a victim of this experiment three times before I was released from this ward to be sent back to the Allan.

#27   The prospect of experimenting on a "normal" unwitting subject generally brought out the scruples of both the doctors and agents – an attitude reminiscent of Nazi doctors tried at Nuremburg. (C. p.56)

Even though an antidote was available it was refused to me each time. It was not in the best interest of the doctor to shorten the duration of the reaction time to the drugs. Otherwise this exercise would be invalid for them and the experiment would be botched. This was another experiment for the furtherance of the medical profession rather than in keeping with the best interests or well being of the patient.

It seemed that each time I was admitted with hepatitis, the hospital duration was for two weeks. Repetitions of all tests and analysis were done each time. Sometimes a different drug was tried, testing to see if there were apparent benefits or negative side effects. After each hospital stay I was always transferred back to the AMI to resume my regular outpatient routine.

Ping-Pong was a game I had once played well. But I never expected to be a human Ping-Pong ball. I found myself bounced back to the Allan. It was here I realized that trying to recuperate was my present career. It was an ongoing somewhat painful struggle. Blood tests and sporadic BSP liver function tests kept the doctor informed on the condition of my liver, and whether or not I was taking all prescribed medication. Psychotherapy, drugs, and daily occupational therapy were the standard methods of treatment at this time.

Spring came and went, and the approaching summer looked promising. My medication was slightly reduced, thus strangely improving my health. I began to feel much better and less lethargic. It was wonderful. Psychotherapy, occupational therapy, and collecting my medication still kept me returning to the Allan almost daily. Sessions with the psychotherapist were not as often as they had previously been. My new status was as a discharged patient yet still within the control and influence of the Allan.

Although the Allan umbilical cord had not yet been completely severed, arrangements for me to go back to school were being made by the hospital Social Services department.

Friends of my family did not object to having me baby-sit their children occasionally. One such friend had an old school mate who needed help. There were complications with her pregnancy and she was confined to total bed-rest until the birth of her twins. Her other two preschool children needed tending during this period. I was asked if I would consider helping her until a reliable person could be hired and I accepted. The twins were born in early May. I stayed there from April until September.

It was a very hectic summer. I learned to cope with the erratic schedules of the babies while at the same time dealing with two very active preschool girls. I survived the summer, and by September my health had improved tremendously. My life was beginning to look brighter. I decided to drop the occupational therapy while I was so busy working with the children. Somehow whenever my medication was reduced, my health seemed to improve. Working helped me feel better about myself.

Life was quite hectic with four little girls. The girls' mother and I were able to function by taking turns with all the feedings, cooking, cleaning, and washing. The grandparents sometimes kept one or both of the older girls for a few days at a time. This made it much easier to cope with the daily routine and the babies.

Whenever the children's grandparents offered to keep the older girls, their mother and I took turns occasionally getting away for a few days. This gave us time to rest while the babies slept. The twins were almost full term and quite large at birth. Caring for them was exhausting but not difficult.

I was still keeping my appointments at the AMI. During one of our sessions, the psychiatrist told me that I would be attending a private high school starting in September. It was required that I first take a few orientation exams given by the provincial government.

I was told that the government was paying for tuition and books and would provide me with a small living allowance. In exchange, I had to live in a supervised environment, take all the medication prescribed, and keep all my appointments at the hospital.

It was a wonderful yet frightening thought to be in a class with a group of unknown and younger students. I did not know how they would react to me because of my age and medical background. Knowing that someone was in a psychiatric ward, or had a mental disorder and was seeing a psychiatrist, was still then a major stigma. And so it was that at the age of eighteen, I was going back to high school.

CHAPTER 19

BACK TO SCHOOL

The Social Services of the RVH placed me at The Centre Maria Goretti. This was a youth hostel for young girls aged eighteen to twenty-eight. Although this was a Catholic institution, many of us were of different religious denominations. This establishment was affiliated with the St. Joseph Oratory but belonged to an Order of the Grey Nuns based in Ontario. It was at the corner of Decelles and Cote Ste. Catherine Road in the Cote Des Neiges area of Montreal. A statue of the young Saint stood above the front entrance, which gave the building the appearance of a seminary for nuns.

The Centre Maria Goretti was a large brick four-storey building situated on the northwest corner. It was diagonally across from the College De Brebeuf, a private school for boys run by the Jesuit Brothers. The reception area and the offices were at the front entrance on Cotes Ste. Catherine Road at the mezzanine level. Glassed private sitting rooms, on the mezzanine to the left side of the elevator, were all accessible to the scrutiny of the nuns from the receptionist's office. Girls who were meeting their boyfriends used these rooms for their visits.

The upper floors featured bright rooms of either single or double occupancy, with a bath, shower, and bathroom facilities at each end of the floors. A large and fully equipped laundry room was located on the second floor. A library and large sitting room were on the lower level. The cafeteria on that floor was available to the general public for three daily meals. The nuns were responsible for the preparation and serving of the meals in the cafeteria. The canteen and recreation centre in the basement were opened until midnight, but boys were not permitted to visit above the mezzanine level.

The Centre Maria Goretti was in the Cote Des Neiges and University of Montreal area, and was used as a recreation centre by young adults. Many of the young nurses working at the Hôpital Ste. Justine were also living in this building, or shared accommodations with other University students elsewhere.

The large canteen had many booths for snacks and light meals for anyone arriving too late to eat at the cafeteria. Many outsiders enjoyed this establishment to socialize, meet friends, and have a light meal. The television was in a corner away from the noises of games such as bowling, ping-pong, and table board games. This was a popular place for young people to mingle.

Nuns taught extra-curricular courses such as ceramics, pottery, music, and religion, which were available for a nominal fee. A Jesuit priest taught theology. Because this centre was opened to the general public, these courses would be advertised in the local paper. Anyone interested could take a course of their choice. These classes were large and well attended, especially the ceramics class, which was very popular in early 1960.

The sitting rooms and the library, which featured a variety of books to excite anyone's imagination, were only for the residents. Residents using these rooms met only with other residents. A few people occasionally practiced on the old upright piano, while others enjoyed the peace and quiet of reading in the comfort of an armchair.

Curfew to enter the building was at 1:00 a.m. Leaving the building after 10:00 p.m. was by permission only. A few misdemeanors could be overlooked, but if the curfew was constantly abused, then the girl would be asked to leave. Because of work schedules, many girls were permitted to enter and then leave with proof of their work hours.

The girls were mostly university students. Some were nurses working at the Hôpital Ste. Justine and a few were working at other jobs in the city. Those coming from different areas of the province, such as Quebec City, usually went home on holidays and days off. During that time the atmosphere in the building was quiet and subdued.

My roommate was a nurse at the Hôpital Ste. Justine. She came from a town about twenty miles south of Montreal. She was working irregular shifts and went home on all her days off. We rarely saw each other. When I was in, she was either sleeping or working, or had gone home. She was unaware that I may have been in a continuously drugged sleep for a few days, or if I was not well.

The nuns were familiar with my health issues and also aware of all my daily medications. I was injecting myself with Gravol three times a day, but a nun had to give me vitamin shots twice a week. I could not understand why I was not allowed to give myself the vitamins as well.

Prescriptions for pills, vitamins, Gravol, syringes, and needles were freely dispensed to me at the RVH pharmacy. If I did not keep the pills down, I was required to then take another dosage. While in the hospital I was often over-dosed with medication, because the hospital staff over-ensured I took my drugs. The result was that I often slept for days at a time until some of the effects of the drugs wore off. Many times I could not tell whether or not I had kept my pills down after eating, or if I had taken them at all.

At last it was September. Emerald green, orange, red, and yellow ochre leaves were the warm colours of late summer adorning the huge trees surrounding the AMI hospital grounds. The weather was sunny and still warm, and we were having a wonderful Indian summer. This gentle transition into the fall season was an exciting and fresh beginning in a new school amongst new acquaintances.

It was both exciting and frightening going back to school after such a long absence. Would I be able to learn again? Could I remember what I had already learned? Many questions and ambivalent feelings raced through my mind. Still it was a very exciting time to which I looked forward.

Ross High School was a private school the government had chosen for me to attend. Within a few weeks I was back to learning. Being away from books for such a long time made me feel a little rusty. Even with all the drugs I was consuming, surprisingly I soon picked up where I had left off. I excelled in geometry, literature, and art. I attended school regularly and enrolled in an extra Saturday morning art class. The only drawback was that I was continuously fighting off sleep and feelings of lethargy. I wanted to decrease the drugs, but was aware that if I did I would jeopardize my continuation in school.

The school's Head Master must have informed the teachers about my condition. No one ever mentioned my lack of alertness in the classroom. Staff members must have wondered why I was so heavily medicated, which was quite obvious by my appearance. I was always tired but still managed to slowly function throughout the day. Eventually after making a few friends, I told them that I was not well. The doctor still prescribed the medication that kept me continually groggy.

Attending school, keeping my appointments, and taking my medicine satisfied my doctor at that time. Everything was going fairly well until my medication was again increased and I became even more lethargic.

Someone was paying for me to attend a private school. Who was the source? Who really paid the bills? There were no documents or receipts. My books were supplied and the government sent me a small monthly living allowance. This had been pre- arranged by the hospital Social Services.

One of the teachers at Ross High was a psychologist who also taught at University. Years later we met socially through friends. He confided to me that he was puzzled by monthly phone calls the school received from someone who enquired as to my progress. When the school asked him if he knew why I was so medicated, he would curtly reply that I was a very sick orphan who had to be medicated because of the nature of my illness. The caller would abruptly hang up so as not to allow an opportunity for further questions.

October arrived, slowly followed by November. The bare trees of autumn had a gray and skeletal appearance. The weather was rapidly changing. Sadly, the warm coloured September leaves had fallen. Now strewn on the sidewalks, they were turning a dirty and muddy brown. The passing clouds contributed to a dull and dismal season in preparation for the cold winter that was only six weeks away.

One Sunday afternoon while going for lunch with friends, we were involved in a small car accident, and were taken to a hospital emergency room. The accident was not serious and I only sustained some bruising and a slight skull fracture. Because my injuries were slight I was released from the hospital a mere few hours later.

The doctor in the emergency ward was appalled when he discovered all the medication I had already consumed that day. It was still early afternoon. He was confused and could not understand how my doctor could prescribe so many drugs to an outpatient. He thought it very unusual. This was his first contact with such a highly medicated individual who was not actually in the hospital.

At the Allan it was time for another change. Three months had elapsed and my time with the psychiatrist had expired. I was resigned to accept variations to my medical regime including a different combination of drugs. My medication was altered, and I continued with the regular psychotherapy sessions with another doctor. At this time each psychiatrist practiced his own method for an individual's treatment. Nonetheless it was always within a guideline set by, discussed with, and approved by his superior, Dr. Cameron.

Each session between a doctor and his patient was recorded. The psychiatrist would record notes taken at each session into a specific telephone in his office. The transmissions from his phone were recorded on a tape to a central machine that was kept behind the receptionist's desk in the lobby. The receptionist would then type each transmission. Dr. Cameron had sole control over this machine and all recordings, irrespective of which doctor convened a session.

Largactil and other familiar drugs were back on my diet. Even with all the medication I was ingesting, and the way I felt as a result, school was still my priority. I tried to attend regularly although I felt ill most of the time. Soon I again began to develop signs of hepatitis. My skin developed a chalky yellow-green pallour. Had I auditioned as a Martian for a movie or a play, I easily would have been given the part. Makeup would not have been required.

Along with my other problems, being anemic made outdoor activities very difficult in cold and damp weather. But I was determined to keep up. I wanted to participate. Sketching out of doors was wonderful when it was warm but I suffered from the extreme cold. Bone pain and colds plagued me. A few weeks later my outdoor sketching plans were defeated due to my weakened health. No more outdoor Saturday art classes for me. Another cold, snowy, and overcast December was coming to an end.

CHAPTER 20

RALPH

The hustle and bustle of Montreal was back to a normal pace after the festive holiday winter season. The weather was my barometer. This typical cold, humid, overcast January reflected how I felt.

Taking the bus to the hospital, I shivered for the entire fourty-five minute trip. Getting off the bus at University Street at the bottom of the hill, I slowly made my way up the sharp incline to the emergency department. The emergency room was always busy. Ambulances were constantly arriving, bringing in people on stretchers. A cross section of people waited to be seen by a doctor. Some remained quietly seated while others were moaning and groaning. It was finally my turn to be seen by a doctor. I was diagnosed with hepatitis once again and admitted to the medical ward at the RVH.

This time we were four to a ward. One of the women was from Newfoundland. She had been born with a rare and severe skin ailment. She was here because of an experimental program that was being tried with new formulated ointments. Twice daily nurses would slather a white ointment all over her body and then wrap her up in gauze. In the evening the nurses removed the gauze, cleaned off the ointment, and then re-applied this sticky white salve before re-wrapping her. She did not object to being covered from head to toe in a thick white ointment, and then rewrapped in gauze like an Egyptian mummy.

At age thirty-five and still unmarried, this woman would sit knitting baby outfits. These were for her nephews, nieces, and anyone else having a baby at home in Newfoundland. All the while she sang happy little ditties. She was always very pleasant, positive, and in a party mood. During her stay on the ward, she met a man who also had a skin ailment. Both would sit and compare their predicament. The ointment that was plastered onto his body was black, and hers was white. Their mutual skin affliction seemed to have brought them together. A few months later they were married.

A Scottish lady with a kidney infection was admitted. She had a special affinity to the patient from Newfoundland, both of whom were pleasant roommates. Despite their severe problems and pain, every afternoon and every evening they would go brew tea in the patients' kitchen. Sitting, drinking tea, and chatting was what they both referred to as "having a party." Both were content as long as they could enjoy a cup of hot brewed tea and a chat. Everything else seemed unimportant.

The other person in our room was an elderly woman. Having suffered a stroke, she was brought in unconscious, and died several days later never having regained consciousness.

A variety of people made up the patient population on this ward. Some were new immigrants and spoke little or no English at all. One such person was a very tall elderly Chinese man whose mouth was filled with gold teeth. His understanding of the English language was minimal. He was a very proud man who nevertheless enjoyed being teased by the nurses. He claimed to have eighty wives in China. Of course, this was unheard of in our society, and it made him that much more of a celebrity.

Back in the ward, each day was a repetition of the previous one. We endured the same routine of blood tests, injections, pills, analysis, various doctors and interns, and more students. Daily life in a ward could be noisy and hectic, especially if some patients were in severe pain. On the other hand it might be a very quiet day, depending on the nature of the illnesses of the patient population.

Nightlife on the other hand was not always tranquil. One of the cardiac patients occasionally became disoriented and climbed out over the protective sides of his bed. If the nurses had difficulty trying to subdue and sedate him so that he would not cause himself harm, they would give him an enema of paraldehyde. Paraldehyde had an instantaneous effect as a sleeping drug. It exhumed an atrocious odour that seemed to permeate the air for quite some distance. But it did keep the patient safe and sleeping, allowing the nurses to continue with their night chores.

I experienced pain, discomfort, weakness, frustration, and anger. With no direction, self-esteem, or pride left, my life was beginning to become a blur. With every clinical rotation, there was a new batch of young interns with different ideas, drugs, and tests. My body was probably suffering from drug abuse rather than hepatitis. Was it really normal for this disease to linger and flare up continuously over such an extended period of time? About two weeks later, along with a batch of drugs and a promise that I would keep my appointments at the Allan, I was discharged from the RVH hospital to again join civilization.

Weaker, thinner, and paler, I attempted to continue with my life. Going back to school was much more difficult than I had anticipated. The medication kept me very groggy so that trying to keep awake was a tremendous effort. It would take time and an alert mind to try to recoup the missed material. Most of the day I spent sleeping at my desk. Unable to keep awake for any prolonged period made it almost impossible for me to absorb what was being taught. It was too difficult to continue. Finally I withdrew and sadly my school days came to an abrupt end.

Back at the Allan as a day patient, the momentum continued at the mercy of the psychiatrist. I was still residing with a roommate at the Centre Maria Goretti. We were two weeks into February when I accidentally took the same medication twice. This time I slept for three days. This was not an isolated experience, since it had happened to me several times before as an in-patient both at the Allan and RVH. Because my roommate worked various shifts at the hospital and went home on her days off, neither she nor anyone else at the Centre was aware that I had been sleeping for three days.

I do not have any memory of those three days. I must have gotten up at some point to use the washroom, although I do not remember having done so. When I did awake after such a bout it was always an ordeal because my blood count suffered. In my weakened state it was very difficult to function well enough to get myself together. It could take almost a full day before I managed to wash, dress, and attempt to comb my hair.

On this particular morning, a nun walking down the hallway found me leaning against a wall. I was groping to support myself as I tried to get to the washroom. In my weakened condition, the effort of walking caused me to blank out every few steps. It was not surprising because I had not had food or liquid during the past three days. She was appalled to find me in such a state. The nuns were aware that I could easily overdose, but were not aware of the frequency of this problem or of what actually occurred during these events.

The simple and basic exercise of washing and dressing was a major chore. Struggling between rests, I did manage to make myself presentable enough to go downstairs for a sandwich and a drink. It was already after 11:00 at night, and the canteen closed at midnight. I had missed my three meals in the cafeteria. I could not get myself ready in time, but at least I did make it for a snack. I even had time before the canteen closed to watch a little television while slowly eating my cheese sandwich.

Almost everyone had left the canteen because it was a weeknight. I had taken my sandwich and drink and slowly made my way to the far corner of the room near the television. I noticed someone sitting on a chair. Eating alone was not enjoyable. Although I was sitting in the row across from that person, I realized I did not feel so alone. The feature movie that night was a murder mystery starring Ida Lupino and Robert Ryan.

As I leaned over to take a bite of the sandwich, I missed a scene on the screen. The loud thumping noise on the television caused me to glance up, but not quick enough to see the action that accompanied the sound. I asked the fellow who was sitting there what had happened. He explained that the loud thump was that of a dead body falling out of the hall closet. I watched a bit more of the movie as I quietly finished my sandwich. The canteen closed, and as we both left I said goodnight to the young man. I slowly made my way back upstairs to my room to rest and recuperate. Unfortunately sleeping became very difficult for me, so throughout that night I just rested and listened to the radio. The next day I resumed taking my pills at the required times. Within a few days I was back to my strange but usual self.

I continued going to the Allan daily for occupational therapy and psychotherapy. The psychiatrist did not seem overly concerned about my recurring overdoses. These occurrences were to be expected and his treatment did not change. I still continued to see him for quite some time. I was no longer attending school. Although I was still weak from taking many pills, my condition had finally stabilized. I was also progressing with my painting in the art room.

The canteen at the Centre Maria Goretti provided an environment where people could meet, chat, enjoy a game of bowling, play a game of Ping-Pong, or sit and watch television. One evening while I was sitting in a booth talking with friends I had met at the Centre, a young man walked over to us. He recognized someone who was sitting with us so he came over to say hello. This was the same person with whom I had sat when I was eating my sandwich a few nights before. Our friends introduced me to Ralph.

CHAPTER 21

AUTOGENIC THERAPY

Days and weeks slowly dragged into months. I was still going for psychotherapy sessions and I obediently continued to take all my medication. Now because of Ralph's concern about my health, I sought the help of a private physician. Not only was this man Ralph's family's doctor, but he was also a very good friend of his family.

The doctor was a big man with thick, dark eyebrows. He was very proud of his shiny bald head which he constantly stroked. When I first saw him I did not know whether or not I would like him. He was a very practical no-nonsense person. He said that it would not be ethical of him to be treating me while I was already in the care of another physician.

At first he did not want to see me for these ethical reasons. Ralph kept pleading and pleading with him. Being as he was on staff at the Royal Victoria Hospital made it possible for him to legitimately pull out and read my patient chart. He was very upset with his findings. According to the chart, not only was I very ill, but I was also being used in experiments. He could not divulge any other details to Ralph. Because he was a personal friend of Ralph's family he felt responsible for Ralph's well being. He advised Ralph to stop seeing me and to find another girlfriend.

Of course Ralph persisted and refused to forget about me. His physician realized that Ralph was serious, so he finally agreed to see me as a patient. With his help over the next year and a half, Ralph helped me cut down safely from all the drugs that I was continuously being prescribed.

#28   Experiments, then may be performed on man, but within what limits? It is our duty and our right to perform an experiment on man whenever it can save his life, cure him or gain him some personal benefit. The principal of medical and surgical morality, therefore, consists in never performing on man an experiment, which might be harmful to him in any extent, even though the results might be highly advantageous to science, i.e. to health of others.... Claude Bernard, 1865.

Under no circumstances is a doctor permitted to do anything that would weaken the physical or mental health resistance of human being except from strictly professional reasons in the interest of his patient.... A doctor is advised to use good caution in publishing discoveries. The same applies to methods of treatment whose value is not recognized by the profession. World Medical Association Declaration of Geneva, 1948, under duties of Doctors in General. (W.p.211)

The psychiatrist could not understand how it was that my condition was improving. I am sure he must have known that I was cutting down on my medication. Since I was no longer a day patient, weekly blood tests to confirm whether or not I was taking my medication were not required. I did go to the hospital regularly for occupational therapy and weekly doctor appointments. Whenever I was asked if I was taking my pills, I would always answer yes. It was not a lie because I was still taking medication, but I did not volunteer any information on how much I was actually taking.

On several occasions the police had delivered truant patients of the Allan to the Verdun Hospital for the mentally ill. Forever present at the back of my mind was the implied threat that I would be sent there if I did not follow the doctor's order. I certainly did not want to be taken there. So I was still in the care of the Allan Memorial Institute, an unpleasant reality with which I had to deal. In the early spring of 1961 I was still not free of illness.

It was time for another change. Research depended on keeping patients within the hospital system. Each doctor was allowed to treat an individual patient for a maximum of three months. I had been under psychiatric care by the same doctor for over three months and our time together was finally up. A reason had to be quickly found to keep me in the hospital system. On occasion doctors conferred with their colleagues to get a different analysis, so that I could be kept on as a patient with a different doctor. Since the doctor who tried to hypnotize me was continuing his research on Rapid Eye Movement in Switzerland, it was not possible for me to be referred back to him at the Allan. I suspect that had I left the hospital it probably would have jeopardized a large percentage of funds to various projects in which the Allan was involved.

A colleague of the referring psychiatrist agreed to take me as one of her patients. "Autogenic Therapy" was a new experimental therapy method. This psychiatrist needed a few more patients to initiate this experiment and felt that many would soon benefit from this exercise. Apparently she was intrigued by the fact that I had persisting and chronic hepatitis, so for some unknown reason I apparently qualified to be part of her new group.

All the patients involved in this project met twice weekly on a regular basis. A space in which to carry out these experiments was set up on the second floor of the stables. It was a tiny, warm, and cozy place in contrast to the high ceilings, cemented floors, and draughty environment of the occupational therapy rooms downstairs. This was more like a small comfortable apartment rather than a doctor's office or laboratory.

Patients were taught Autogenic Therapy. This was a new technique on achieving total relaxation. For most of the time during these sessions, patients practiced self-hypnosis while coaching one another. This helped to establish and control the time, duration, and focus of the exercise. Each session ended with the doctor heading a group therapy discussion before we dispersed. Most of the patients had previously been subjected to ECTs, which were often emotionally threatening. This non-threatening therapy was a pleasant relief.

Autogenic Therapy is a form of total relaxation practiced through breathing and focusing on different areas and parts of the body. One concentrates on imagining each limb becoming hot or cold, heavy or light. Through thought, the brain controls each part of the body separately or as a whole. Thinking controls the action. The procedure was to last no longer than three minutes. Breathing skills practiced at the beginning of each session were different from those methods at the session's end. Apparently not ending with the proper breathing technique was dangerous.

These sessions lasted three months. All the while I was still seeing the psychiatrist regularly for psychotherapy. My treatment at the AMI with all those doctors remained the same, with only the medications being varied. At this time the drugs Phenobarb and Phenobarbital were added. I doubt that the doctor was aware that I was cutting down on my pills. I never did confide this information to her. She never questioned whether or not I took my medication.

CHAPTER 22

THE END OF AN ERA

Social events at the AMI were held every Saturday evening when either a current movie was shown or lectures were given. The hospital did try to have interesting and varied programs to stimulate and encourage the patient population. Patients, families, and friends were encouraged to attend. Professors, doctors, artists, or other qualified people gave free lectures. The variety of subjects appealed to different patients every week. Movies and travelogues were also popular. Discussions were encouraged after each event.

Ralph accompanied me to some of these Saturday evening lectures. One speaker was a member of the famous Canadian "Group of Seven" artists, and a very good friend of the hospital's art therapist. He was among one of many lecturers. Tall and lean, with yellowing white hair almost to his shoulders, this young senior hippie captivated his audience. He regaled in the presence of people, especially children and women. He had charisma and charm. At the end of the lecture he was often seen pinching some of the young women as they walked past. Today that would be called sexual harassment, but then it was most tolerated. Some women were even delighted that someone might pay attention to them.

The art therapist encouraged me to enroll in the Teaching Art classes at The School of Art and Design, affiliated with the Museum of Fine Arts. This was in September of 1961. I was still in the system at the AMI and seeing a psychiatrist for psychotherapy.

The government supported me as long as I was connected to the Allan. In December of 1961 I decided to leave the Centre Maria Goretti and share an apartment with two girls. Splitting the expenses and maintaining the apartment worked out very well. I also did some evening babysitting to supplement my allowance, so that I could purchase new clothing and small luxuries. My expenses were less than at the Centre because here I could cook meals rather than eat at restaurants.

Most of the experiments on Autogenic Therapy had recently been completed and the doctor seemed pleased with the results of her project. All the patients in the group had dispersed. A few of us were still involved with her singularly for psychotherapy sessions.

Ralph's physician was now seeing me weekly and still supervising the types and amounts of drugs that I could ingest. My health was gradually improving. I was coping with the courses and teaching practicum at the museum. I was spreading out psychotherapy appointments to fit my schedule with the school program. Ralph and I saw each other so often that his doctor jokingly suggested that we marry.

From September 1961 to May 1962, I attended the museum and completed the teaching course. I kept most of my appointments with the psychiatrist, who was unaware that by May I was no longer taking medication. In April I started working part-time in a day care centre and a few months later became a full-time teacher. Ralph and I were planning to marry in June of 1962.

I submitted myself to one final EEG in May, helping the psychiatrist prove that her theory about Autogenic Therapy exercise was successful. The findings were favourable and were recorded and published. That was my final appointment at the AMI. I walked away. I was free. The threat that the police would come after me to institutionalize me or send me to the Verdun Hospital for the mentally ill had no validity.

I walked away from that hospital. It had been a painful and long three and a half years. No more hepatitis, or vomiting, or drugs. I was normal except for the black pin marks, like giant tattoos, that were still visible in the inside crease of each elbow. The threat of being sent to Verdun was empty. It was merely a means of control so that I would not do what I had just done, to walk away free and without fear. On June 9, 1962, Ralph and I were married.

From 1976 to 1978, I suffered from the effects of histoplasmosis. This was not discovered until 1978. Vomiting blood and severe chest pains were symptoms of a possible ulcer, so whenever I experienced these symptoms I would go to the emergency at the Montreal Jewish General Hospital. Each time a tube was inserted through my nostril to my stomach to drain the blood. A blood test always confirmed internal bleeding but the source was never found. It was not coming from my stomach.

A chest x-ray also showed scarring on my lungs. After each x-ray I was asked when I had had tuberculosis. I have never had tuberculosis. Provincial licensing for any public facility required everyone working with children in a daycare, or serving meals, to have a yearly chest x-ray and blood test. It was mandated by a Quebec provincial law not to allow anyone suffering from communicable diseases, such as tuberculosis, to be permitted to work in daycares.

After another gastroscopy and a few more x-rays, my physician still did not have any idea what was wrong with me. He sent me to a surgeon to make sure that he had not missed anything in his testing. The results were inconclusive and baffling once again. Doctors did not know what they were looking for and were puzzled.

Severe cutting pain through my chest was cause for another night spent in the emergency of the Jewish General Hospital. Again, x-rays were taken, showing that my lungs were scarred. Once again a technician inquired as to when I had had tuberculosis. Once more my answer was that I never had tuberculosis and could not understand why this was happening. This diagnosis was a complete mystery.

A urologist was requested to see me because I was passing stones. Although the stones had passed from the kidneys, apparently they were not true kidney stones, but were typical of someone who had had tuberculosis. This was very strange and puzzling. When could I have possibly had TB?

Another approach was needed. There had to be an answer to my unusual symptoms. We had to determine if these problems were physical or psychological. So, to have another objective opinion, it was suggested that I see a psychiatrist.

An appointment was made for me in early 1977 to consult the psychiatrist I had last seen in

1962. Although fifteen years had elapsed, she recognized me and was amazed that I had not changed. She recalled that she had accepted me as her patient at the Allan in 1961, and decided to review old personal patient files to refresh her memory. According to her I really was not ill. At that time Autogenic Therapy was a new theory with which she was experimenting. She needed a certain number of patients in order to ensure secure funding for her program. I had to be kept within the system as a patient, but with a different doctor, so she had agreed to take me.

At my next appointment with her, the doctor told me that my file had mysteriously disappeared. She could not understand how this could have happened, because to her knowledge no one else had access to her files. I saw her only once more. My physician was satisfied that it was not necessary to continue seeing a psychiatrist.

What had happened to my files? Many years later some former patients of the AMI filed a class action suit against Dr. Ewan Cameron and the CIA. Someone suggested that I contact a lawyer in Washington D.C. who was representing the plaintiffs. I provided the lawyer with my personal medical information. I was informed that although there was evidence on file of my time spent at the Allan, including medications and treatments prescribed, most everything had been shredded. There was not enough information, evidence, or proof to hold up in court. This final insult was the end of an era.

CHAPTER 23

STARTING OVER

In the summer of 1978 my husband and I went on a pilot trip to Israel. We had family ties in Israel and many of our friends had already left Quebec to live there. We wanted to see if we too could emigrate with our four children, and decide whether or not it would be a good choice for them if we moved there.

These friends were happy with the changes they had made for themselves and their children. Although the change of lifestyle and learning to speak a new language was a challenge, it was an improvement for their sense of family unity. Living on a kibbutz created for them a larger family unit with the members. It eliminated the financial and emotional stresses that they had experienced in Canada of having a large family. There was more in the way of extra-curricular activities, such as educational courses, art classes, and horseback riding for themselves as well as their children.

Things that were not affordable for them in Canada were readily available on the kibbutz.

We met with many people and traveled throughout the country. This was not an easy decision for us to make. We decided that it really was not what our family needed. It would not be easy for our children to adapt to so many changes.

For our boys it would be a tremendous culture shock and not in their best interest to be uprooted. They were already in high school and the drastic change of the language, school, and being removed too far from their friends, would be too traumatic. The girls were still quite young and adjusting might have proved much easier for them.

Although English is heard in Israel, Hebrew is the working language of the country and of education. For our high school aged boys, one of whom was diagnosed with audio-visual dyslexia, a totally different language and different school system was not in their best interest. It would make them very unhappy, so we decided to move to western Canada instead. At least the language would not be a barrier and they would still be learning in a Canadian school system.

During our visit to Israel, the symptoms of my illness mysteriously and miraculously vanished. Possibly it was the hot, sunny climate, or maybe whatever ailment I suffered from had finally run its course. We traveled throughout Israel visiting people and places, and looking into job and housing opportunities. At that time our plans were either to immigrate to Israel or move west to Calgary, where Ralph already had employment starting that September.

On our return to Montreal, we purchased a Volvo station wagon for our journey across the country. It was a memorable trip for all of us, camping and picnicking along the way. Sometimes we stopped in little towns to purchase the local produce, see the people, and learn the history of the area. Most of the time we camped, encouraging the children to pick berries to have with pancakes in the morning, or to try fishing in the narrow streams. This was an enjoyable time for us all and is still fondly remembered by our children.

Calgary welcomed us with its quirky weather. We arrived to horrific thunder clasps and a massive hail thunderstorm that finally subsided into a blanket of rain. With the Bow River flash flooding and the rain pounding on the roof of the car, we quickly decided to drive on through to British Columbia. The company that had hired Ralph was on strike. We decided that since we had already come this far west, why not continue to Vancouver? Until the strike was settled in Calgary, we could visit with Ralph's parents who were already living in North Vancouver. We had previously made arrangements to have our belongings put in storage in Calgary and insured until September. This was August and we did not have to be anywhere specifically for another three weeks.

British Columbia was spacious, lush, green, and warm. We arrived on the Sunday that Abbottsford was having its annual air show. The sun was shining, the people were friendly, and we all felt positive about this province. We decided to stay rather than return to Calgary.

That lush green landscape, the ocean, and the relaxed, passive lifestyle made it impossible for us to return to the uncertain climate of Alberta. The extreme weather in Quebec was also a factor that encouraged us to leave the east. Our family happily settled in British Columbia, where at least the seasons would not be as extreme or unpredictable as they were in Alberta.

At the time of our arrival, Richmond was a township of approximately 92,000 people. It was quiet and looked like a good place to raise the children. Richmond is three feet below sea level and surrounded by a dyke. Unlike Montreal, Richmond has no hills. Children riding bicycles to school did not worry their parents because the traffic was minimal. Richmond was an extreme contrast to Montreal and, we thought, an ideal place to raise a family.

Living in the west and leaving the east meant starting over. Within a few months we were orientated enough to find an area in which we could easily adapt. Ralph did not have a problem finding employment. We found a family doctor and a dentist who were compatible with our family needs. Now we could concentrate on becoming B.C. citizens.

One day, after a routine chest x-ray, it was discovered that the mysterious disease that had plagued me in Montreal was called histoplasmosis. It baffled everyone in Montreal, but was easy to detect in B.C. Apparently many people in Montreal are unaware that they have this disease.

Histoplasmosis is a fungal infection contracted by breathing in spores. The spores are usually from bird droppings and distributed through dust after the demolition of an old building. At one time this disease was called "The Curse of the Pharaohs" because many people became ill and died after digging in the old Egyptian tombs.

Montreal was suffering from the demolition hype of the 1960's and 1970's. Unfortunately a large number of older establishments, including many heritage buildings, were destroyed in the name of progress. A great deal of dust was produced every time a building was torn down. The dust carried the spores in the air. That is probably how I contracted histoplasmosis in the first place. Walking by a demolition site, or simply by spending time outdoors, I was probably breathing in spores.

After marriage and children, I still continued slowly with my education. I already had an art-teaching certificate as well as certification from the School of Art and Design. I acquired kindergarten-teaching qualifications at the Thomas Moore Institute and completed high school through adult education in Montreal. Throughout the years I have also taken other courses at random at Kwantlan College in Richmond, B.C.

I developed a technique for apple sculpture and had a few successful exhibitions. A professor of opera at the University of British Columbia commissioned me to provide him with a collection of apple sculptured doll characters. These were based on the Comedia del L'Arte, Shakespeare, and some opera personalities such as Othello and Desdemona.

In the meantime, Ralph and I have a happy marriage. Our four children and nine beautiful grandchildren continue to give us much pleasure.

Although my life has been forever affected by my experience, I have learned to live with and accept my present state of health and have moved on. I will not dwell in the past, but neither will I forget.

BIBLIOGRAPHY

A Father, a Son and the CIA
by Harvey Weinstein
Publishers James Lorimer & Company
Toronto,   1988

# 7	#21
# 9	#26
#10	#28

IN THE SLEEP ROOM   by Anne Collins
Publishers   Lester & Orpen Dennys
Copyright @ Anne Collins, 1988

# 1	#13	#20
# 4	#14	#22
# 5	#15	#23
# 6	#16	#24
# 8	#17	#25
#11	#18	#27
#12	#19	

THE WORLD'S WORST MEDICAL MISTAKES
MARTIN AND KAREN FIDO
Published by Sevenoakes Limited 1996

# 2	# 3